Office of Juvenile Justice and Delinquency Prevention

The Office of Juvenile Justice and Delinquency Prevention (OJJDP) was established by the President and Congress through the Juvenile Justice and Delinquency Prevention (JJDP) Act of 1974, Public Law 93–415, as amended. Located within the Office of Justice Programs of the U.S. Department of Justice, OJJDP's goal is to provide national leadership in addressing the issues of juvenile delinquency and improving juvenile justice.

OJJDP sponsors a broad array of research, program, and training initiatives to improve the juvenile justice system as a whole, as well as to benefit individual youth-serving agencies. These initiatives are carried out by seven components within OJJDP, described below.

Research and Program Development Division develops knowledge on national trends in juvenile delinquency; supports a program for data collection and information sharing that incorporates elements of statistical and systems development; identifies how delinquency develops and the best methods for its prevention, intervention, and treatment; and analyzes practices and trends in the juvenile justice system.

Training and Technical Assistance Division provides juvenile justice training and technical assistance to Federal, State, and local governments; law enforcement, judiciary, and corrections personnel; and private agencies, educational institutions, and community organizations.

Special Emphasis Division provides discretionary funds to public and private agencies, organizations, and individuals to replicate tested approaches to delinquency prevention, treatment, and control in such pertinent areas as chronic juvenile offenders, community-based sanctions, and the disproportionate representation of minorities in the juvenile justice system.

State Relations and Assistance Division supports collaborative efforts by States to carry out the mandates of the JJDP Act by providing formula grant funds to States; furnishing technical assistance to States, local governments, and private agencies; and monitoring State compliance with the JJDP Act.

Information Dissemination and Planning Unit informs individuals and organizations of OJJDP initiatives; disseminates information on juvenile justice, delinquency prevention, and missing children; and coordinates program planning efforts within OJJDP. The unit's activities include publishing research and statistical reports, bulletins, and other documents, as well as overseeing the operations of the Juvenile Justice Clearinghouse.

Concentration of Federal Efforts Program promotes interagency cooperation and coordination among Federal agencies with responsibilities in the area of juvenile justice. The program primarily carries out this responsibility through the Coordinating Council on Juvenile Justice and Delinquency Prevention, an independent body within the executive branch that was established by Congress through the JJDP Act.

Missing and Exploited Children Program seeks to promote effective policies and procedures for addressing the problem of missing and exploited children. Established by the Missing Children's Assistance Act of 1984, the program provides funds for a variety of activities to support and coordinate a network of resources such as the National Center for Missing and Exploited Children; training and technical assistance to a network of 43 State clearinghouses, nonprofit organizations, law enforcement personnel, and attorneys; and research and demonstration programs.

OJJDP provides leadership, direction, and resources to the juvenile justice community to help prevent and control delinquency throughout the country.

Juvenile Intensive Supervision: Planning Guide

Program Summary

Barry Krisberg
Deborah Neuenfeldt
Richard Wiebush
Orlando Rodriguez

National Council on Crime and Delinquency

John J. Wilson, Acting Administrator
Office of Juvenile Justice and Delinquency Prevention

Foreword

OJJDP considers the intensive supervision program (ISP) a promising intermediate sanction for first-time serious or violent juvenile offenders who are inappropriate for or fail to respond successfully to immediate intervention. Many serious and violent offenders at this stage may be appropriate for placement in an intensive supervision program that serves as an alternative to secure incarceration. The Intensive Supervision of Probationers Program Model is a highly structured, continuously monitored, individualized plan that consists of five phases with decreasing levels of restrictiveness:

1. Short-term placement in community confinement.

2. Day treatment.

3. Outreach and tracking.

4. Routine supervision.

5. Discharge and followup.

Program models such as these have been found to be effective for many serious, violent, and chronic juvenile offenders, obviating the need for secure incarceration. OJJDP views the intensive supervision program as a positive response to the need to address the overcrowding of juvenile detention centers. The *Planning Guide* offers practitioners the tools they need to implement confidently an ISP as an alternative to long-term institutional confinement for designated juvenile offenders.

OJJDP believes the intensive supervision program offers the juvenile justice system a needed alternative to incarceration for the right juvenile offender.

John J. Wilson
Acting Administrator
Office of Juvenile Justice and Delinquency Prevention

Acknowledgments

The authors gratefully acknowledge the cooperation of the administration and staff of the sites visited in preparing this report and the support and counsel of the project advisory board: Judge David Grossmann, Hamilton County, Ohio, Juvenile Court; Peter Greenwood, RAND Corporation; Douglas Lipton, Narcotic and Drug Research, Inc.; and Cal Terhune, California Youth Authority. Finally, we convey our appreciation to Yitzhak Bakal, Northeastern Family Institute, Inc., and Thomas Lynch, New Jersey Division of Juvenile Services, for their review of the program model.

Table of Contents

Foreword ....

Acknowledgments v

Introduction 1

  Goals 1

  Juvenile intensive supervision... 2

  Rationale 2

  Key elements 3

  The manual 4

Program context 5

  Philosophy 5

  Theoretical framework 6

Client identification.. 9

  Target population 9

    Definition 9

    Baseline planning study 11

  Selection procedures and criteria 13

    Policy 13

    Screening process 14

    Selection alternatives 20

Phases of the intensive supervision model 22

  Context 22

  The phase system 23

    Policy 23

    Phase 1. Residential or institutional placement 24

    Phase 2. Day treatment... 25

    Phase 3. Outreach and tracking (reintegration)............. 28

    Phase 4. Regular supervision (transition) 29

    Phase 5. Discharge and followup 30

Program components 31

  Case planning and management 31

    Policies 31

    Case assessment 32

    Strategies for juvenile supervision................................. 33

    Case planning 35

    Objectives-based contracting 37

Reassessment 39

Program rewards and sanctions 39

    Policy 39

    Operational strategy 39

Program services 44

    Overview 44

    Direct vs. brokered services 45

    Service areas 45

    Core services 45

    Supportive services 51

Summary 52

Context and implementation 52

External environment 52

    Administrative support 53

    External support 54

Program linkages 58

Internal linkages 60

    Conditions 60

    Operational issues 61

Summary 66

Goals and evaluation 66

Demonstration goals 66

    Program goals 66

    Program objectives 67

Management information system 68

    Overview 68

    MIS design 68

    Data elements 71

Evaluation 73

    Process evaluation 73

    Outcome evaluation 75

Conclusion 76

References 77

Program sites visited by NCCD 79

List of Figures

Figure 1   Integrated Strain-Control Paradigm 7

Figure 2   NCCD Juvenile Classification Scale 12

Figure 3   Michigan Youth Services Rates of Subsequent
Rearrest by Risk Group 14

Figure 4   Michigan Youth Services Delinquency Risk Assessment Scale 16

Figure 5   Alaska Youth Services Needs Assessment Scale 17

Figure 6   ISP Selection Matrix 19

Figure 7   Operational Alternatives for Screening and Selection 21

Figure 8   Core Intervention Strategies 23

Figure 9   Prior Permission Rules 26

Figure 10   Force Field on Probationer Henry Ward 36

Figure 11   Sample Case Planning Format 38

Figure 12   Michigan Youth Services Risk Reassessment: Scale
Community Supervision 40

Figure 13   Violation Categories and Appropriate Sanctions (example) 42

Figure 14   Lucas County (Toledo), Ohio, Juvenile Court 44

Figure 15   Supervision—Control Components by Phase 47

Figure 16   Agency Management Process 69

Introduction

Burgeoning court systems and overcrowded juvenile facilities prompt interest in programs that provide serious juvenile offenders with community-based intensive supervision as an alternative to confinement. Responding to this need, the Office of Juvenile Justice and Delinquency Prevention (OJJDP) funded "Postadjudication Nonresidential Intensive Supervision Programs," a project conducted by the National Council on Crime and Delinquency (NCCD).

Goals

The project goals are:

- To identify and assess operational or effective intensive supervision programs.

- To provide the capability to selected localities to implement effective intensive supervision programs for serious offenders through intensive training and technical assistance.

- To disseminate effective postadjudicatory, nonresidential intensive supervision program designs for supervision of serious juvenile offenders.

Project activities to meet these goals comprise four steps:

- Stage One — Assess existing programs and information.

- Stage Two — Develop a comprehensive program manual.

- Stage Three — Develop training and technical assistance materials.

- Stage Four — Provide training and technical assistance to selected sites.

Stage One assessment consisted of a literature review and nationwide search for promising juvenile intensive supervision programs (ISP's). NCCD selected 11 programs for extensive site visits. NCCD found great diversity among ISP's. Assessment of existing ISP's indicates that while there is potential in the use of intensive supervision for juvenile offenders, more quantitative outcome data are needed about these programs. Strengths and weaknesses were evident in all programs studied, and no complete model emerged. NCCD, therefore, developed this manual to capitalize on the observed strengths of current programs and further refine other program components.

The findings of the Stage One assessment can be found in two project reports available through NCCD:

- *Selected Program Summaries* includes complete site reports for the 11 programs.

- *Assessment Report* includes the literature review and methodology along with the findings and recommendations.

> Overcrowded juvenile facilities prompt interest in community-based intensive supervision.

Research indicates intensive supervision is as effective as incarceration in reducing recidivism.

This manual specifies the elements of a good ISP based on the knowledge gained during the assessment process. It also provides operational requirements and, where appropriate, alternatives for model implementation. Technical assistance and training materials are now being developed to support implementation of the program described in this manual.

Juvenile intensive supervision

Intensive supervision programs encompass a wide variety of programs and strategies. Although more prevalent in the adult correctional system, ISP's programs targeted at serious offenders are gaining popularity in juvenile justice systems throughout the country. The definition of juvenile offender varies among programs. For example, the chronic juvenile offender refers to the individual who began his or her delinquent career at an early age, has numerous minor offenses, and for whom regular probation has been ineffective. ISP's can work for those juveniles who have committed more serious but nonviolent offenses as well.

Juvenile ISP's are community-based programs characterized by high levels of contact and intervention by the probation officer or caseworker, small caseloads, and strict conditions of compliance. Juvenile ISP's are designed as an alternative to institutionalization. Some programs include treatment/services components, while others emphasize surveillance and controls.

Although juvenile ISP's can be defined in many ways (depending upon the goals of the individual jurisdiction), for the purposes of this project we have defined ISP as postadjudication, nonresidential programs for serious juvenile offenders as an alternative to long-term institutional placement.

Rationale

The program model described in this manual is based on the premise that high-risk youth can be safely and effectively managed in the community after their behavior has been stabilized. The literature on intensive supervision for juveniles, while limited, indicates that intensive supervision programs are at least as effective as incarceration in reducing recidivism (Krisberg et al., 1989; Barton and Butts, 1988; Krisberg et al., 1988; Murray and Cox, 1979; Coates et al., 1978; Lerman, 1975; Empey and Lubeck, 1971). The Barton and Butts study concluded that the intensive supervision programs provided a significant savings in the cost of juvenile corrections; the cost of ISP was estimated to be less than a third of the cost of commitment.

The ISP model recognizes that youth identified as serious or high-risk offenders come from troubled backgrounds and have already established rather lengthy or serious delinquent histories. Previous actions by the court (fines, restitution, and probation) have met with limited success. For intensive supervision to be effective, it must be substantially different from these earlier interventions.

The development of an effective model of intensive supervision for high-risk juvenile offenders has significant ramifications. If an intensive supervision program for juveniles proves effective, society gains on three fronts:

■ Youth remain in an environment in which they must learn to live, rather than being removed to an artificially controlled setting where programs may be more dependent on environment than actual changes in attitudes.

■ Cost of care is contained. Juvenile incarceration has proved enormously expensive, often approaching (and in some cases exceeding) $50,000 per case per year. Even the most expensive community-based programs are less costly.

■ Unnecessary facility construction is avoided. Crowding, inadequate physical facilities, and insufficient treatment capabilities are problems throughout the juvenile justice system, with little attention from policymakers because of the increased focus on the adult correctional system crisis. The number of incarcerated youth could decline if effective alternatives exist on a wide-scale basis.

Key elements

Key elements in the program model are summarized briefly here. The remainder of the manual is organized around these five key elements.

Program context. The ISP strategy described in this model is guided by both theory and professional experience. The model is based on a philosophy of risk control, which incorporates incapacitation and rehabilitative goals. Accountability is also stressed. The combination of supervision and services defined in the model is in keeping with the framework of the Integrated Social Control Theory of Delinquency developed by Elliott et al. (1985).

Client identification. The primary target population for the ISP is adjudicated delinquents committed to State or local correctional institutions because of the seriousness of their offenses or their risk of continued delinquent activity. Proper identification and selection procedures to ensure that a correctional facility-bound population is served by the program is the single most important element in implementation of the model. A baseline study to determine the characteristics of committed youth and use of structured decisionmaking instruments are strategies for proper selection that will be discussed.

Intervention strategy. Given the troubled youth that this program intends to serve, the model requires a comprehensive effort that encompasses highly structured supervision and a broad array of treatment alternatives. This effort includes a phased system of controls, case planning and continuous case management, core service requirements, and a system of rewards and graduated sanctions. The five program phases under the model are (1) short-term residential placement or incarceration, (2) day treatment, (3) outreach and tracking, (4) routine supervision, and (5) discharge from supervision.

For intensive supervision to be effective, it must be distinct.

A monitoring and evaluation system enhances cost effectiveness.

Contextual and implementation issues. The design supports the philosophy that an ISP will be most effective when it has a broad base of ongoing community support and is used in conjunction with other community resources. The comprehensive program of supervision and services requires the coordinated efforts of multiple agencies. Variations in both the external environment and the internal organizational structure of agencies implementing the model will have an impact on certain operational decisions and must be considered carefully.

Goals and evaluation. Because of the comprehensive nature of the ISP design, the cost of this program will be considerably more than traditional probation. If used as probation enhancement for juveniles who would not otherwise be placed out of home, the model would likely be prohibitively expensive for many jurisdictions. However, it is our expectation that the program will be cost effective when compared with the expense of most residential placements. An evaluation design to test these premises will be discussed.

The manual

This manual has several purposes. First, it describes in detail a program model for intensive supervision for serious juvenile offenders. The model was developed following an extensive assessment process, and we believe it offers great promise as an effective community-based alternative to residential placements. In addition to describing the program model, this manual serves as a resource for agencies interested in developing their own intensive supervision programs. The manual provides a structure for the consideration of the basic issues involved in the development of juvenile ISP's and provides the theoretical rationale for the design.

The manual also lays out key monitoring and evaluation issues to be considered during project design. All too often, these issues are ignored in implementation efforts, and subsequent questions from policymakers and funding sources about who is being served and the cost effectiveness of the program remain unanswered. Designing a monitoring and evaluation system as part of program development generally proves more cost effective than expensive retrospective studies.

Although further training and technical assistance may be necessary for full implementation, the manual is intended to serve, at minimum, as an important first step in local program design.

The manual is organized according to the five key program elements described above. Where the model is prescriptive, the rationale for the requirement is explained. Where organizational flexibility within the context of the model is appropriate, operational options are provided. Examples of program forms used in other jurisdictions are provided as well.

Although this manual is designed to serve as a guide, it is strongly recommended that a jurisdiction implementing the model develop its own agency-specific operational manual as part of any development effort.

The back of this manual lists the 11 intensive supervision programs to which NCCD made onsite visits during the assessment stage. These programs invested considerable time to provide program materials. Their successes and struggles in implementing intensive supervision for serious juvenile offenders contributed greatly to NCCD's efforts. Concrete examples from these programs are given throughout the manual.

Program context

Program context is defined as the set of conditions and assumptions that operationally and conceptually define the distinctive features of the program model. This set includes the program philosophy and the theoretical assumptions guiding the model.

Philosophy

Policies and procedures for ISP's are to be guided by the risk control philosophy, which incorporates rehabilitation and incapacitative goals. Although the model addresses other correctional goals, such as accountability (via a restitution component, for example), the approach presented here focuses primarily on risk control and rehabilitation rationales.

Under the risk control approach, the central purpose of a sanction is to prevent the offender from committing future criminal acts. Sanctions are influenced by the seriousness of the present offense, but are primarily based on the offender's potential for continuing delinquent activity (risk). Thus, the degree of control should be commensurate with the predicted potential for future delinquent activity. This also implies that the degree of control should not be excessive; each sanction should be graduated to the potential for future delinquency.

Risk control justifies the higher than normal supervision costs involved in ISP's through its payoff in increased control over the offender's behavior (Clear, 1986). Although debate continues within the juvenile justice system over how increased control should be defined, intensive supervision programs generally achieve control through smaller caseloads, increased frequency of contacts, the use of surveillance (including unannounced visits at home and work), preventive conditions, and the ability to impose swift and certain consequences for violation of the program conditions (O'Leary and Clear, 1984). These are incapacitation strategies.

Risk control also emphasizes rehabilitative goals. Although ISP was created as a response to the perceived need for greater monitoring of offenders' behavior, few juvenile justice programs operate without rehabilitation components. For example, among 11 model ISP's examined (Krisberg et al., 1989), only 2

> Under the risk control approach, the central purpose of a sanction is to prevent the offender from committing future criminal acts.

Weak bonding to family, school, and community can lead to a delinquent lifestyle.

relied strictly upon incapacitation approaches, such as monitoring and surveillance. The other programs emphasized the importance of education, job training, life skills counseling, involvement with community activities, and the development of long-term goals for youth. Rehabilitative efforts are fundamental to the risk control approach, because reducing the likelihood of future offending is contingent upon affecting change in cognitive, emotional, and behavioral patterns (Clear, 1986).

An important factor dictating inclusion of rehabilitative components in ISP is the need to fill clients' time with positive activities. The tools of incapacitation—surveillance, monitoring, deprivation—work best in correctional institutions. Because intensive supervision is an intermediate sanction between incarceration and regular probation, ISP clients live, work, and study in the community. In an ISP, participation in education programs, job training, and other rehabilitative interventions is seen as a necessary complement to monitoring. These activities fill offenders' time (thus serving as a risk control strategy) and also have the potential of producing alternative rewards to criminal activity.

Theoretical framework

ISP interventions should address the major causal factors identified in delinquency theory and research, most aptly explained by Elliott et al. (1985) in the Integrated Social Control (ISC) model. In planning the program, each intervention should be justified by its hypothesized effect on one or more of the delinquency causation factors, and each factor should be represented by at least one intervention.

The ISC approach integrates the central components of control, strain, and social learning theories. It argues that the combined forces of inadequate socialization, strains between occupational and educational aspirations and expectations, and neighborhood social disorganization lead to weak bonding to conventional values and activities in the family, school, and community. Weak bonding can lead youth to a delinquent lifestyle through negative peer influences. Figure 1 outlines the Integrated Strain-Control Paradigm.

Each major explanatory factor is examined below:

Social disorganization. In the ISC model and other conceptualizations, some social environments engender subcultures with attitudes and perceptions conducive to delinquency and other deviant behaviors.

Socialization. In the context of the family, patterns of supervision and discipline established by parents in early childhood are seen as causally relevant to delinquency. In childrearing, parental discipline may be absent, inadequate, or may rely on physical punishment. Parental skill deficits may also be apparent in terms of moral reasoning, consistent application of rewards and sanctions, and problems and crises. Conditions such as abuse, neglect, violence, or substance abuse may be present as well. These socialization experiences may prevent the development of strong external bonds (e.g., to the family) and internal bonds (e.g., self-discipline) (Fagan et al., 1984).

Figure 1: Integrated Strain-Control Paradigm

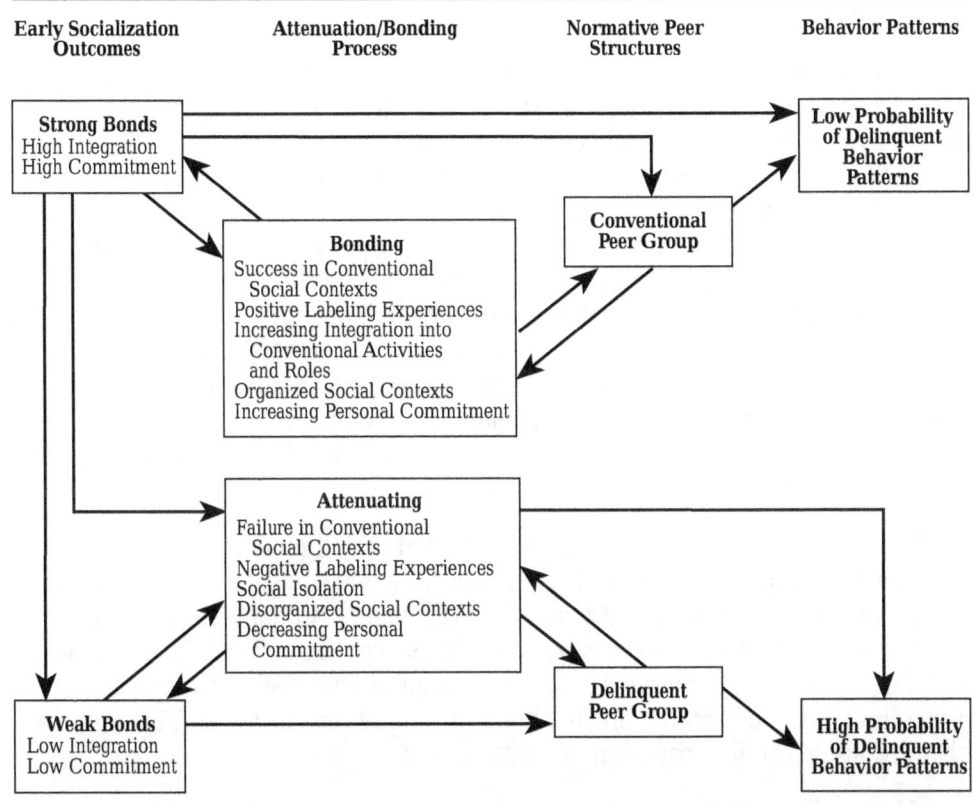

| Early Socialization Outcomes | Attenuation/Bonding Process | Normative Peer Structures | Behavior Patterns |

Strong Bonds
High Integration
High Commitment

Bonding
Success in Conventional
   Social Contexts
Positive Labeling Experiences
Increasing Integration into
   Conventional Activities
   and Roles
Organized Social Contexts
Increasing Personal Commitment

Conventional Peer Group

Low Probability of Delinquent Behavior Patterns

Attenuating
Failure in Conventional
   Social Contexts
Negative Labeling Experiences
Social Isolation
Disorganized Social Contexts
Decreasing Personal
   Commitment

Weak Bonds
Low Integration
Low Commitment

Delinquent Peer Group

High Probability of Delinquent Behavior Patterns

Strain. This factor refers to the social-psychological process by which one's disadvantaged social status causes antisocial behavior. From this perspective, delinquency is seen as an outcome of discrepancies between achievement aspirations and expectations. For example, if a youth aspires to college, but does not expect to achieve this either because of perceived blocks to opportunities or self-doubts, delinquent behavior is a way of coping with the frustration of failure.

Conventional bonding. The ISC model views the above factors as precursors to delinquency in that they may result in a lack of conventional bonding with the family, school, and other social institutions that bind youth to traditional values and rules. When conventional bonding is effective, youth develop emotional attachments to the school and family, commitment to conventional activities, involvement in such activities, and belief in the moral order underlying conventional bonds.

Peer bonding. The outcome of interaction between peers is critical in explaining delinquent behavior. Delinquency is influenced by one's peers through the same social-psychological mechanisms that operate in conventional bonding, namely, emotional attachment, commitment to, and involvement in peer activities arising from socialization by delinquently inclined peers. Adolescents learn delinquency by exposure to their friends' law-violating behavior, peers' social approval for delinquent acts, and anticipated rewards for engaging in delinquency. Peer group influences on delinquency are especially likely when there is weak bonding to the family and school.

Self-esteem. Another potentially important factor covered in the ISC model, which should also be considered in ISP interventions, is personality characteristics related to the notion of self-esteem (Kandel, 1974; Kaplan, 1975; Kaplan et al., 1984). Most programs design interventions that implicitly focus upon motivational variables, such as self-esteem. These factors operate at three levels. At the individual level, negative self-concept directly influences antisocial involvements. At the social group level (i.e., the family, school, and peer group), negative outcomes of interaction with such groups (e.g., school failure) influence antisocial involvement and also influence a negative self-concept. At the societal level, the quality of the neighborhood environment and the effect of occupational/educational opportunities available to the youth indirectly influence delinquency by producing strain and affecting the ability of the family and other social groups to foster conventional bonds with the adolescent.

ISP's have to address each of the factors related to delinquency causation. By their nature, programs have most direct control over the youth's actions, less on family and peers, and practically no effect on social disorganization and socialization (because important socialization effects occur in early childhood). However, the planned ISP interventions should spell out how each etiological factor, regardless of the program's practical control over it, is addressed. This implies that programs should propose interventions that:

- Have a direct impact on the client, for example, reducing strain by providing educational or job opportunities, and enhancing self-esteem.

- Have a direct impact on the client by enhancing his/her ability to successfully cope with negative influences of neighborhood social disorganization, family, or peers.

- Have an indirect impact on the client through actions aimed at the family, peers, or community.

For example, although a program may not be able to influence directly clients' delinquent friends, it could propose counseling programs that are intended to enhance clients' self-esteem and at the same time reduce their motivation to socialize with delinquent friends.

It should be noted that the ISC model is a theory of delinquency among the general adolescent population and the applicability of its major factors to institution-bound youth should be considered carefully. For example, the model assumes that involvement with the family keeps adolescents from delinquent involvement. From this, it would follow that a program would wish to promote clients' involvement with their families. However, with seriously dysfunctional families, this could be counterproductive and interventions might better focus on ways of building the youth's strengths and coping abilities.

Client identification

Client identification is defined as the combination of techniques, criteria, and procedures used to define, select, and admit participants to ISP. There are two major aspects of client identification. The first aspect is defining the target population: Who is it that ISP seeks to serve? The second aspect is the selection procedures and criteria that ensure that those identified in the target population are selected for participation.

Target population

Definition

The target population for the ISP model is postadjudication delinquents who would otherwise be in a State or local juvenile correctional institution for at least 12 months[1] because of the seriousness of their offenses or their risk of continued delinquent activity.

The ISP model is designed to serve as an alternative to correctional placement for serious offenders. This model assumes that these youth can be safely and effectively served in the community after their behavior has been stabilized. This chapter will explain the rationale for identifying this target group and discuss procedures to ensure that the target population is, in fact, selected.

Types of offenders. What types of offenders are included in this definition? Under the rubric of serious offenders are two types that should be targeted for ISP participation—chronic offenders and those who have committed serious but nonviolent offenses. Chronic offenders have committed multiple offenses, typically including status as well as delinquent offenses. They are likely to have been on probation and to have failed—to have not met the conditions of their probation and to have committed new offenses. Often, previous programs or treatment have been tried to no avail. Short-term detention or residential treatment may have been used, but the offenses and perhaps running away continued. The offense resulting in correctional placement may not be that serious, but the pattern of offenses and lack of success in the community have led to commitment. When structured risk assessment instruments are used, these chronic offenders tend to score high on risk of reoffending.

The second group for ISP includes serious but nonviolent offenders—those who have committed serious property crimes, including drug trafficking. These youth are less likely to recidivate than the first group; however, the seriousness of their offenses has led to correctional placement. Some of these juveniles may be inappropriate for ISP because the nature of the offense demands a primarily punitive response (i.e., secure placement). Many States specify by law waiver to the adult court system or training school placement for certain offenses. Except for specific crimes, serious offenders should not be automatically excluded from ISP. Instead, juveniles committed to correctional placements should be screened for the program, using the structured assessment tools described in a later section.

---

[1] Or at least the average length of stay in the State training school if less than 12 months.

> **P**rograms benefit by focusing on ways to build youth's strengths and coping abilities.

Although it is necessary to identify those individuals who are not appropriate for the program because of factors such as violent offenses or special needs, care must be taken that exclusionary criteria are not used in such a way to refocus the target population on minor offenders. Rather than establishing specific exclusionary criteria, an override procedure, detailed later in this chapter, should be established to document these factors.

Implications. Ensuring selection of this target population for the ISP is the single most important element in the prototype implementation. Why is the appropriate target population so critical to this model design? Target group selection impacts program and cost effectiveness. ISP's widen the net when they impose stringent controls on youth who otherwise would be placed on regular probation; hence the rationale to target juveniles who would otherwise be in a correctional institution. In addition, program capacity for controlling the true target population is reduced when ISP's try to provide control not warranted by the juvenile's offense or risk to the community.

Further, ISP may not be as effective as regular probation for low-risk offenders. A study of the Second District Juvenile Court of Utah (NCCD, 1987) suggested that more intensive supervision for low-risk offenders did not produce better results than regular probation. Evaluations of adult ISP's have shown similar results. Although ISP is more successful than regular probation for high-risk offenders, some studies (Erwin, 1986; Markley and Eisenberg, 1986; Andrews, 1987) have shown that low-risk offenders actually fare worse in ISP than regular probation. This result occurs because the more intense scrutiny and more stringent conditions of ISP supervision result in technical violations that would not have been caught under regular probation. If low-risk offenders who would not otherwise be in a residential placement are selected for the program, ISP may actually exacerbate institutional crowding, rather than help alleviate it (Clear and Hardyman, 1990).

Cost effectiveness is also significantly improved by proper target group selection. ISP is significantly more expensive than regular probation. Without proper selection of the ISP target population, the program would be prohibitively expensive for most jurisdictions.

ISP's selected for assessment under Stage One of this project target youth who would otherwise have been in residential programs (only the Lucas County, Ohio, program exclusively targeted youth who would otherwise be in a training school). Although this target group was generally agreed upon within each ISP, the programs differed in their definitions of who might be placed in a residential program. NCCD found no uniform definition of high-risk, serious, or chronic offender that applied across ISP's or, often, within ISP. An individual youth's appropriateness for the program was determined through intuitive staff judgments. No program used structured risk or need instruments for assessment or program screening. The programs had little objective data to show that the ISP population met the target group criteria. As a result, it was difficult to assess whether there was departure from the intended target population. The informality and lack of documentation of the selection procedures leads us to believe that many ISP's informally expand their target population. This factor is a major problem that NCCD addresses through several means: (1) the baseline study described below; (2) use of structured screening procedures, including use of risk assessment instruments; and (3) strict management control.

Baseline planning study

To fully understand the potential of a program to divert offenders from juvenile institutions, preprogram profiles of institutional populations should be generated. The proportion of potential diversion cases is directly related to each jurisdiction's use of institutional placements. Since sentencing practices and placement resources vary substantially, the number and types of offenders potentially eligible for ISP will not be the same across jurisdictions. Examples exist of both adult and juvenile ISP's that have targeted an institution-bound population only to discover that the eligible pool was too small to maintain a viable program. A baseline planning study will help to determine whether there are enough institution-bound youth who are eligible for the program. The baseline study can also identify potential groups of offenders for various alternatives and help refine the selection criteria. Finally, when the baseline data are later compared with postprogram profiles, the ability of ISP to truly divert institution-bound youth can be determined.

This approach has been used in various States, including Utah, Massachusetts, Colorado, and Wisconsin. The Wisconsin study (Baird and Neuenfeldt, 1989) was designed to determine whether a significant proportion of the Wisconsin juvenile incarcerated population could be safely and effectively supervised in community-based programs. Information was collected on a random sample of juveniles admitted in 1986 to Wisconsin's two training schools. The data showed that 68 percent of the juveniles were incarcerated for nonassaultive offenses and 59 percent had no history of violent offenses.

A structured classification instrument was developed, similar to those used in Colorado, Delaware, and Oregon, that determined the seriousness of the committing offense, the offense history, and other juvenile risk factors, such as drug and alcohol use, history of mental health services, and runaway history. The NCCD juvenile classification scale developed for the Wisconsin study is shown in figure 2.

The instrument classified the juveniles into three groups: (1) youth adjudicated for serious violent offenses and those with extreme chronic delinquency histories who would require secure placement; (2) youth adjudicated for property offenses with limited histories of delinquency who would be appropriate for community placement; and (3) youth who fall in between the community and highest security levels. For this in-between group, a period of short-term secure placement was recommended for further diagnostic purposes and to serve as a needed intervention, to be followed by a community placement or program.

Using the classification instrument, the study estimated that only 27 percent of the Wisconsin incarcerated juveniles required long-term secure placement, while 26 percent were appropriate for direct community placement and 47 percent were appropriate for short-term secure care, followed by community placement. The study further found that the profile of incarcerated juveniles

A baseline study can identify appropriate offenders for various alternatives.

The classification instrument was not designed to be used as a screening device, but as a planning tool.

varied considerably by county, indicating that there was considerable disparity among counties in the types of youth sent to State facilities. Although youth from Milwaukee County (by far the largest county in the State) were, overall, more serious offenders, only 35 percent of the Milwaukee County juveniles met the criteria for secure care. These findings, similar to findings in other jurisdictions, suggest that there is a large pool of potential diversion cases in Wisconsin. It should be noted that the classification instrument example shown in figure 2 was not designed to be used as a screening instrument, but rather as a planning tool. Examples of case-specific assessment instruments are presented in the next section of this report.

Researchers strongly recommend that a similar baseline study take place during ISP planning. Information should be collected on the characteristics of a sample of incarcerated juveniles, including risk profiles, offense profiles, and prior attempts at intervention. Analysis of the data will give an indication of the potential pool of cases for ISP. Those youth whose high scores indicate serious offense histories or extensive prior interventions would not be considered appropriate for ISP. The remainder of the youth could be considered a pool of potential ISP candidates.

Figure 2: NCCD Juvenile Classification Scale

	Score
1. Severity of Current Offense	
Murder, Rape, Kidnapping	10
Other Offense Involving Use of a Weapon or Use of Force	5
2. Most Serious Prior Adjudication	
Any Offense Involving Use of a Weapon or Use of Force	5
No Priors or Property Only	0
3. Number of Prior Out of Home Placements	
Three or More	5
Two or Less	0
Total Items 1–3	_____

Total Items 1–3. If score is 10 or higher, secure placement is recommended. If less than 10, score the remaining items.

4. Prior Placement in a Juvenile Correctional Institution	
Yes	2
No	0
5. Age at First Delinquent Adjudication	
14 or Under	2
15 or Over	0
6. History of Mental Health Outpatient or Drug/Alcohol Care	
Yes	1
No	0
7. Prior Runaways	
Three or More	1
Two or Fewer	0
Total Items 1–7	_____

Recommendations:

10 or Above:	Secure Placement
5–9:	Short-Term Secure Care
0–4:	Community Placement

Those youth with the lowest scores (appropriate for community placement) pose certain questions. Why are these juveniles in long-term placement? Individual assessments may well identify reasons not adequately captured on the baseline planning instrument. However, if large numbers of juveniles fall into the lowest category, placement policies may be questioned. Second, is placement of this group in ISP an optimum use of system resources? As noted previously, program effectiveness may be compromised if a low-risk population is served. Selecting low-risk, institution-bound juveniles for ISP may help meet institutional reduction goals, but the real solution lies in revised placement policies using objective criteria to avoid inappropriately placed juveniles in the first place.

Selection procedures and criteria

Policy

ISP youth will be selected from those committed to an institutional placement on the basis of risk of subsequent delinquent activity or the seriousness of the current offense. Criteria will be explicitly defined and consistently applied to all cases through the use of a structured decisionmaking tool. Staff input will determine overrides to the indicated placement, but overrides will be carefully monitored by management to prevent net-widening.

The timing of the selection procedures is crucial to achieving the target population as designed. As the most effective way to secure proper target group selection, the model requires that screening for ISP acceptance occur after court sentencing to an institutional placement. As the Barton and Butts study (1988) demonstrated, even this approach does not ensure that net-widening will not occur. Without the selection process occurring after an initial commitment decision, the evidence suggests that it would be extremely difficult to avoid going beyond the intended ISP target population.

Rationale for policy. Use of a structured decisionmaking tool is essential to ensure that specific factors are considered for all cases by all staff in a consistent manner. Consistency in the screening process is the only way to ensure that the criteria established by policy for target group selection are adhered to during program implementation. Use of such instruments also provides a way to document deviations in selection policies. This use also will enable evaluators to determine the extent of and reasons for the discrepancies. Are juveniles being screened out at a high rate? What reasons are given? Who is making the decision (ISP staff worker, judge, screening panel)? Without a structured instrument to show who met the objective criteria, it would be impossible to say whether these decisions are consistent with the stated program goals and policies.

At minimum, the following instruments should be used during the participant selection process: risk assessment, needs assessment, and program selection matrix. Rationales for the use of these instruments will be discussed and sample instruments given.

Youth with serious offense histories or extensive prior interventions would not qualify for intensive supervision.

T he actuarial risk assessment instrument is more accurate than clinical predictions.

Screening process

Risk assessment instrument. Risk assessment is a procedure for estimating the probability that a juvenile offender will commit another crime. Two basic approaches to risk assessment can be applied—clinical and actuarial. Clinical assessments are based on interpretation and judgment of staff, often a single individual. Actuarial assessments are based on the statistical relationship between behavior and characteristics and the outcome measured. Clinical assessments are plagued by a lack of reliability in that they lack consistency among raters. Although they often require high levels of expertise and time, clinical predictions are less accurate than actuarially based instruments (Meehl, 1954)[2]. Therefore, an actuarial risk assessment instrument is recommended as a primary basis for the ISP screening process.

The actuarial approach is based on group predictions. The risk assessment divides the delinquent population into groups that have different base rates of recidivism. Well-designed risk instruments provide maximum separation of these subgroups based on actual rates of recidivism; the highest risk group will have much higher rates of recidivism than the lowest risk group. A rule of thumb is that the highest risk group should fail at the rate of at least four times the rate of the lowest risk group. As an example, figure 3 shows the rates of rearrest of risk groups referred by or committed to Michigan Youth Services. (Risk levels were calculated using the risk instrument shown in figure 4.)

Because risk assessment instruments are based on group data, they are effective in predicting aggregate outcomes. However, the instruments will not correctly predict outcomes for all individuals; some high-risk offenders will never commit another crime, and some low-risk offenders will reoffend. Therefore, risk assessment should be viewed as a decisionmaking tool. It is a way to reduce our uncertainty about human behavior, but it can never eliminate uncertainty (Clear, 1988).

Figure 3: Michigan Youth Services Rates of Subsequent Rearrest by Risk Group

Risk Level	Number of Cases	Once	Percent Rearrested Twice	Thrice	Total
Low	331 (33%)	11.2%	3.6%	0.3%	14.8%
Moderate	511 (51%)	28.8%	7.6%	2.9%	39.3%
High	156 (16%)	28.8%	16.7%	7.1%	52.6%
	998 (100%)				

[2]NCCD recommends that research be conducted to determine the effectiveness of the ISP in dealing with serious juvenile offenders. The preferred approach is an experimental research design, with random assignment to the program of those committed juveniles determined appropriate for ISP. A State-administered program would provide the best opportunity for this approach.

Most research indicates two types of variables that are related to criminal activity—prior criminal history and stability factors. Not surprisingly, the best predictors of future behavior are the recency, frequency, and severity of past criminal behavior. Therefore, criminal history items such as the number of prior arrests or adjudications and age at first arrest or adjudication are often included on delinquency risk instruments. In addition, stability items like substance abuse problems, school problems, and prior out-of-home placements are also strongly related to recidivism.

Because the delinquents assessed for ISP are serious and chronic offenders, screeners would also like to measure another risk: What is the risk that a juvenile will commit a violent act? Because the rate of violence (even among the ISP population) is low, predicting violent or assaultive behavior is extremely difficult. As a result, most risk assessment scales are not designed to predict violence. Recidivism is easier to predict because minor or moderately serious offenses occur more frequently, and a prediction that a new offense of any type will or will not be committed is far less specific than predicting violent behavior. Although the risk scale does not, therefore, predict the likelihood of future violent acts, the decision matrix and override procedures discussed later take into account previous violent offenses in determining the delinquent's appropriateness for the program.

Ideally, a jurisdiction developing a risk assessment instrument would conduct research on its delinquency population to determine what factors are directly related to recidivism within the jurisdiction. If local research is not an option, a sufficient body of research has been conducted throughout the country to enable a jurisdiction to develop a risk instrument. If a jurisdiction adopts an existing risk assessment instrument, the instrument should be validated with the jurisdiction's delinquent population.

The Michigan Office of Children and Youth Services recently conducted a study of all delinquents committed or referred to the State juvenile correctional agency for care and supervision. Because this population is similar to the target population of ISP, the risk scale developed for Michigan is an appropriate example for ISP model. Figure 4 presents the Michigan risk scale.

Needs assessment instrument. In addition to the risk assessment, a structured needs assessment will be completed to determine client needs. This assessment provides for consistency and uniform consideration of needs areas. Unlike the risk instrument, the needs assessment is not used to structure the program admission decision. Rather it is used to ensure that certain problem areas are examined each time for each juvenile. It screens cases to identify those with severe needs that may require further indepth assessment and may result in program rejection. After program acceptance, needs assessment results are used in case planning to identify the appropriate program or service needs of an ndividual youth. A structured, formalized needs assessment will do the following:

■ Ensure that certain types of problems are considered for all cases and aid in formulating a case plan.

S creeners who assess chronic offenders seek to determine the risk that an offender will commit a violent act.

The best predictors of future behavior are the recency, frequency, and severity of past criminal behavior.

Figure 4: Michigan Youth Services Delinquency Risk Assessment Scale

		Score
1.	**Age at first adjudication**	____
	11 or under 3	
	12–14 2	
	15 1	
	16 or over 0	
2.	**Number of prior arrests**	____
	None 0	
	One or two 1	
	Three or more 2	
3.	**Current offense**	____
	Nonassaultive offense (i.e., property, drug, etc.) 2	
	All others 0	
4.	**Number of prior out-of-home placements**	____
	One or fewer 0	
	Two or more 1	
5.	**History of drug usage**	____
	No known use or experimentation only 0	
	Regular use, serious disruption of functioning 1	
6.	**Current school status**	____
	Attending regularly, occasional truancy only,	
	or graduated/GED 0	
	Dropped out of school 1	
	Expelled/suspended or habitually truant 2	
7.	**Youth was on probation at time of commitment to DSS**	____
	No 0	
	Yes 1	
8.	**Number of runaways from prior placements**	____
	None 0	
	One or more 1	
9.	**Number of grades behind in school**	____
	One or fewer 0	
	Two or three 1	
	Four or more 2	
10.	**Level of parental/caretaker control**	____
	Generally effective 0	
	Inconsistent or ineffective 1	
	Little or no supervision provided 2	
11.	**Peer relationships**	____
	Good support and influence; associates with	
	nondelinquent friends 0	
	Not peer-oriented or some companions with	
	delinquent orientations 2	
	Most companions involved in delinquent	
	behavior or gang involvement/membership 3	
	Total Score:	____

Risk Assessment
- 0–8   Low risk
- 9–13   Moderate risk
- 14–18 High risk

- Provide an additional measure for setting priorities (i.e., judging the amount of effort that should be expended on an individual case relative to the entire caseload).

- Provide a base for monitoring a juvenile's progress.

- Force qualitative review of every case through periodic reassessments and provide a basis for judging the relative effectiveness of the case plan and casework approach.

- Provide a data base for planning, monitoring, and evaluation of the program.

A nationwide review of juvenile corrections' needs assessment instruments shows that they are generally quite similar in content and format. Unlike risk assessment instruments, needs assessments are not predictive scales and are rarely the results of statistical analyses. Instead, needs assessment instruments are usually developed by staff in an effort to articulate and formalize case assessment procedures through a structured process of identification, definition, and prioritization of problems frequently encountered in clients. The needs assessment instrument developed by Alaska Youth Services is presented in figure 5 as an example. Case assessment procedures following program acceptance is discussed more fully in the intervention chapter.

A review of juvenile corrections' needs assessment instruments reveals similar content and format.

Figure 5: Alaska Youth Services Needs Assessment Scale

	Score
1. Basic Living Situation	_____
Suitable living environment 0	
Stable out-of-home residence 2	
Transitional residence problems, three or more settings 3	
Chronic residence problems, nomadic lifestyle, unacceptable residence 6	
2. Primary Family Relationships	_____
Relatively stable or not applicable 0	
Some disorganization or stress, but potential for improvement 2	
Chronic disorganization or stress with some potential for improvement 3	
Major chronic disorganization or stress 6	
3. Alternative Family Relationships	_____
Relatively stable relationship or not applicable 0	
Some disorganization or stress but potential for improvement 2	
Chronic but moderate disorganization or stress 3	
Major chronic disorganization or stress 6	_____
4. Emotional Stability	_____
Appropriate adolescent responses. No apparent dysfunction 0	
Marginal adolescent responses. Minor reluctantly responds to expectations and directions 2	
Exaggerated periodic or sporadic responses such as aggressive acting out or depressive withdrawal 3	
Excessive responses prohibit or limit adequate functioning 6	

5. **Peer Relationships** _____
Adequate social skills and nondelinquent friends 0
Negative friends or socially inept 2
Delinquent peers 3
Exploitive or manipulative peers or self; and most activities
with groups having strong delinquent orientation 6

6. **Substance Abuse** _____
No known use or interference with functioning 0
Experimentation but no indication of sustained use 1
Occasional use/abuse, some disruption of functioning 2
Chronic abuse, serious disruption of functioning 4

7. **Victimization** _____
No history or indication of physical or sexual abuse 0
Suspected physical or sexual abuse or sexual exploitation 1
Verified physical abuse 2
Verified sexual abuse or both 4

8. **Intellectual Ability** _____
Ability to function independently 0
Average or above measured intelligence but has educational
disability 1
Mild retardation requiring need for some assistance 2
Deficiencies severely limit independent functioning 3

9. **School Adjustment** _____
Attending, in correspondence, graduated, GED. No history of
discipline problems 0
Occasional attendance, work effort or disciplinary problems
handled at home/school level 2
Severe truancy, behavior problems or failing to maintain
grade level standing 3
Not attending, withdrawn or expelled 6

10. **Employment** _____
Not needed or currently employed 0
Currently employed but poor work habits 1
Needs part-time employment to pay restitution 2
Needs employment full- or part-time 3

11. **Vocational/Technical Skills** _____
Currently developing marketable skill or not applicable 0
Needs skills/attending school 2
Needs vocational training 3

12. **Transportation** _____
Adequate transportation is available 0
Transportation is unavailable or inadequate 2

13. **Health/Hygiene and Personal Appearance**
Enter the value "1" for each characteristic which applies to this case.
Medical or dental referral needed
Needs health or hygiene education _____
Appearance and self-sufficiency skills needed _____
Handicap or illness limits functioning _____

Total Need Score (1 Through 13): _____

Program selection matrix. The decision to accept a juvenile into ISP should be based on objective criteria. This can be accomplished through the use of a program selection matrix, which contains the salient factors considered in determining appropriateness for program participation. Generally, these factors include risk of recidivism and offense history. Low-risk youth with limited offense histories would be recommended for traditional probation. (Because the population screened consists of youth committed to long-term institutional placements, few youth should be in this category. How to handle those few committed youth who are appropriate for regular probation would depend on the operation of the juvenile justice system. For example, in States where judges control ISP admission, ISP staff would recommend that the court rescind the commitment order and order probation instead.) High-risk youth with multiple violent offenses would be recommended for incarceration. Those in between would be recommended for ISP. An example of a possible ISP selection matrix can be found in figure 6.

Of course, an actual matrix should reflect each jurisdiction's unique laws, definitions, and policies. It is important to note that decisions concerning what factors and which programs to include in the matrix are policy decisions that reflect a strong consensus among key juvenile justice decisionmakers.

What factors and which programs to include in the matrix are policy decisions.

Figure 6: ISP Selection Matrix

Committing Offense / Offense History	Low	Moderate	High
Major Violent and Multiple Violent Offense[1]	Institutional Placement	Institutional Placement	Long-Term Institutional Placement
Violent Chronic Offense[2]	ISP/ Institutional Placement	ISP/ Institutional Placement	Institutional Placement
Violent Chronic Offense (single violent episode)[3]	ISP/Probation	ISP	ISP/ Institutional Placement
Serious Chronic Offense[4]	ISP	ISP	ISP
Nonserious Chronic Offense[5]	Probation	Probation	ISP
Nonserious Nonchronic Offense[6]	Probation	Probation	Probation

[1]Murder, rape, kidnapping, or history of violent offenses (e g , two+ aggravated assault)
[2]Instant offense is violent (robbery, aggravated assault); no other violent, but five or more delinquent offenses
[3]Instant offense is violent (robbery, aggravated assault); but less than five or more delinquent priors
[4]Instant offense is violent (burglary); and has five or more priors
[5]Instant offense is nonserious (theft); and has five or more priors
[6]Instant offense is nonserious (theft); and has less than five priors

No set of
instruments can
capture all the
information about
an individual.

Override procedure. There are two types of overrides—discretionary and policy. Discretionary overrides occur when it is determined that the circumstances of a case warrant a different placement than is called for on the program selection matrix. A good override procedure must document in writing the reasons for the departure from the matrix. Reasons may include the extreme violence of the offense or extraordinary needs that can best be handled in a residential setting, such as the need for inpatient mental health treatment. No set of instruments can capture all the information about an individual, and the professional judgment of ISP staff (caseworker and supervisor) will determine when exceptions are necessary.

Policy overrides occur when ISP staff make a decision contrary to the one that the decision matrix indicates. For example, the NCCD model does not allow for the consideration of low-risk juveniles with limited offense histories for ISP. If youth meeting this profile have been committed to State training schools, a mechanism should be in place to change the inappropriate commitment order. If change is not possible, diversion to ISP may be considered a policy override. These cases, however, are not the target group for ISP, and their results should be reported separately.

Overrides need to be closely monitored. Generally, overrides should not exceed 15 percent of the total decisions. A higher override rate indicates problems with the decisionmaking instruments or indicates problems with staff acceptance of the system.

In ISP's where staff do not have final control over program acceptance, documentation of judicial overrides should also be maintained. If these become excessive, the discrepancies should be discussed with the court to resolve the problem.

Selection alternatives

The statutory structure of a State's juvenile justice system will impact on the operational design of the screening and selection procedures. Figure 7 illustrates two operational alternatives, although it recognizes that each State's juvenile justice system has unique characteristics and variations on these two approaches.

Youth authority State. In States where a State corrections agency (youth authority) controls placement and release after commitment, the State agency would administer ISP. The baseline study would determine the jurisdictions in the State that have a deficient number of offenders eligible for ISP. Once operational, screening for ISP could occur at a State juvenile reception center or at a local secure care facility.

Judicial authority State. In States where judges place and release juveniles, ISP staff would screen youth after a commitment to a State or local correctional institution, but before the actual transport. After the ISP screening to determine eligibility and appropriateness for the program, recommendations

Figure 7: Operational Alternatives for Screening and Selection

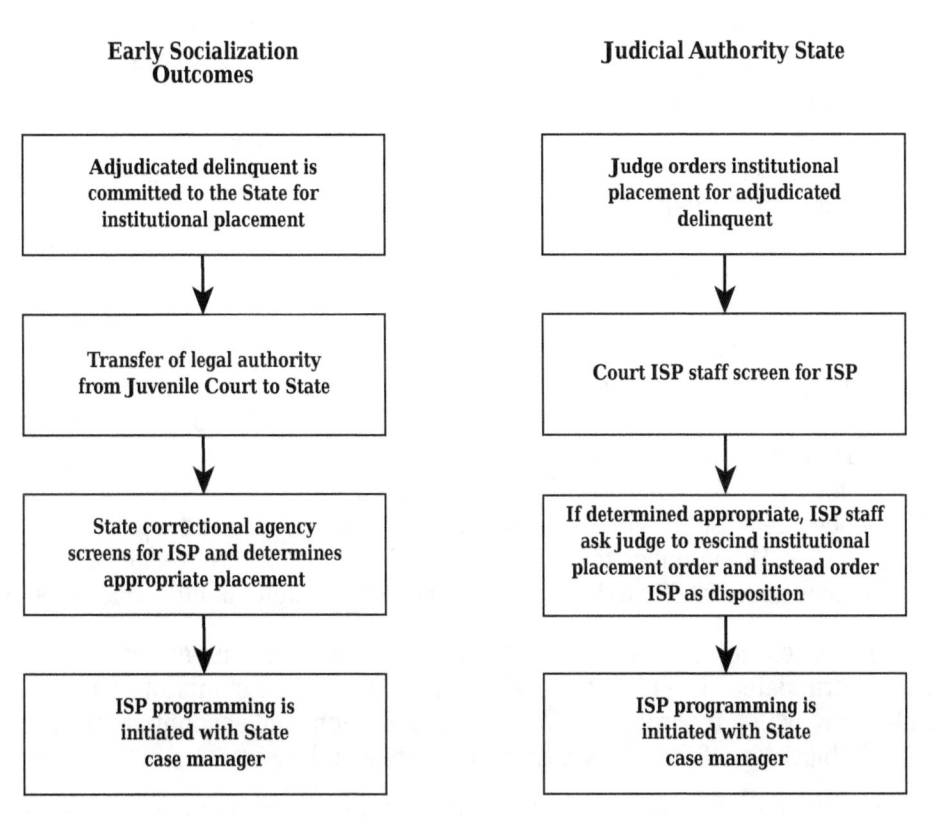

Early Socialization Outcomes	Judicial Authority State
Adjudicated delinquent is committed to the State for institutional placement	Judge orders institutional placement for adjudicated delinquent
Transfer of legal authority from Juvenile Court to State	Court ISP staff screen for ISP
State correctional agency screens for ISP and determines appropriate placement	If determined appropriate, ISP staff ask judge to rescind institutional placement order and instead order ISP as disposition
ISP programming is initiated with State case manager	ISP programming is initiated with State case manager

The commitment of juvenile judges to the program is essential.

concerning program acceptance would be made to the court for a modification to the institutional commitment order. Decisions contrary to the presumptions established by the screening criteria will be documented as overrides of the selection procedures.

Under this scenario, the final decision for program participation rests with the court designee. The commitment of the juvenile judges to the program model, communication between ISP staff and judiciary personnel, and proper training in the program model and procedures are essential to ensure that the court and program staff have a common understanding of the program criteria and procedures.

In summary, the proper target group identification and selection procedures are crucial elements in the ISP model design. Steps to ensure proper screening and selection must be built into the program after an institutional placement has been ordered. These steps should proceed the use of structured decisionmaking instruments, including structured risk and needs assessments and program acceptance criteria based on uniform factors.

Phases of the intensive supervision model

The purpose of this chapter is to describe the context for the intervention model described in chapters 3 and 4 and to explain the five program phases. The focus will be on the principles that should guide program design and implementation. Even though these principles are derived from prior research and the experiences of the most successful programs, new efforts must adapt these guidelines to local circumstances and available resources.

Context

As outlined in chapter 1, the Integrated Social Control theory suggests that youth become involved in delinquent behavior because of weakened bonds to conventional values, persons, and institutions. The lack of involvement in positive behavior may be a result of several factors, including early socialization experiences, psychological development, social disorganization, and the strain experienced because of the discrepancy between aspirations and legitimate opportunities. When bonds to legitimate social institutions are weakened, youth may become socialized to a delinquent orientation through the influence of peers.

Given these causal factors, a number of objectives for an intervention model can be formulated. The objectives reflect the theoretical assumptions and a philosophy which incorporates control, rehabilitation, and accountability. The central objectives of the intervention model are as follows:

- Provide direct external control over the offender until the locus of control can be shifted to traditional socialization units, such as the family, school, place of employment, or ultimately, to the offender.

- Mitigate the effects of inadequate socialization and social disorganization by reestablishing or strengthening offender bonds to conventional values, persons, activities, and institutions.

- Address strain and self-esteem issues by providing youth with the skills and opportunities to be successful in traditional settings.

- Provide a consistently applied system of reinforcements (rewards and sanctions) to support desirable behaviors and to reduce the influence of the delinquent peer group as a criminogenic force.

These objectives can be translated into a set of intervention strategies that will guide program design and operations. These core strategies are summarized in figure 8. They are intended to apply to multiple areas of service delivery. For example, the relationship-building strategy would apply to people within the program (e.g., case managers, surveillance officers), to service providers (e.g., substance abuse counselors), to the youth's family members, and to employers or teachers. Similarly, the use of graduated and consistently applied rewards and sanctions should not be restricted solely to program staff, but should also be applied by parents, teachers, and others involved with the youth.

The next section discusses the policies, purposes, and programming of each of the five program phases.

Figure 8: Core Intervention Strategies

1. Operate a phase system characterized by an initially high level of external program control to be progressively decreased as the offender displays a greater level of responsibility and internal controls.

2. Deliver or access a range of services guided by a continuously monitored individualized case plan.

3. Develop a constellation of relationships among the youth and law-abiding persons, groups, and institutions that can provide alternative role models, a source of rewards and sanctions external to the program, a network of community support, and a vehicle for disengagement from delinquent peer groups.

4. Teach youth the social and interpersonal skills necessary to maintain positive involvement with family, school, work, prosocial peers, and community institutions.

5. Develop youth competence in life skills, education, and employment.

6. Arrange and advocate for access to opportunities in education and employment that provide meaningful rewards in the short term and long term.

7. Address individualized risk factors that impede functioning or that have weakened the youth's prosocial attachments.

8. Consistently apply graduated rewards and sanctions that recognize youth achievement, and provide immediate accountability for violations.

The initial phase will entail the greatest control over the offender.

The phase system

Policy

A formal phase system consisting of five distinct levels will structure the youth's movement through ISP. The initial phase will entail the greatest level of control over the offender, with subsequent phases reflecting decreasing levels of restrictiveness.

The five phases and their anticipated duration are:

Phase 1.   Residential or Institutional Placement—15 to 45 days.

Phase 2.   Day Treatment—4 to 6 months.

Phase 3.   Outreach and Tracking (Reintegration)—3 to 4 months.

Phase 4.   Regular Supervision (Transition)—2 to 3 months.

Phase 5.   Discharge and Followup—1 to 2 months.

A significant amount of time is required to change the behavior of serious offenders.

Movement through the phases is based upon the youth's need for a controlled environment, responsiveness to each phase, and attainment of treatment goals for each phase. Each phase, however, has a prescribed minimum length of stay.

Rationale for policy. The primary assumptions behind a phase structure are that a graduated approach to full community reintegration is necessary to ensure public safety and to allow consolidation and testing of positive behavior before movement to a less restrictive phase. Related assumptions are that: (1) youth who would have been committed to a correctional institution will initially require a high degree of external control both to stabilize their behavior and to ensure public safety; (2) the possibility of attaining greater freedom in subsequent stages is a motivating factor to full program compliance or participation; and (3) through effective and staged program interventions offenders will gradually assume greater degrees of responsibility for themselves.

The specified duration of each phase and the entire program is based upon the experience of existing programs and the nature of the goals sought for each stage (detailed below). The approximate 10- to 15-month duration of the entire ISP reflects the notion that, even with intensive services, a significant amount of time is required to change the behavior of serious offenders.

Phase 1. Residential or institutional placement

Purposes. This initial program period should be 15 to 45 days after court commitment. The primary objectives of this phase are (1) stabilization of the youth's behavior, (2) orientation to program rules and expectations, (3) detailed assessment of the youth's need for control and services, and (4) development of a comprehensive service plan. This highly restrictive phase could also be seen as a way to hold the youth accountable for the offense committed.

Location. Where phase 1 participants are held will vary by the type of jurisdiction implementing the program, the size of the program, and other factors. In State-operated or large locally operated programs, the initial period might be spent in a staff-secure, community-based residential facility designed for ISP. Alternatively, such jurisdictions may opt to designate one unit of a reception or diagnostic facility as the ISP unit. (This assumes that 10 to 15 ISP youth would be in phase 1 at any given time.) Where the size of the ISP would not warrant a separate unit or facility, it is likely that phase 1 participants would be housed in a local detention facility.

Programming. Services during phase 1 focus primarily on orientation, assessment, and case planning. The juvenile and his or her family should be provided with a detailed explanation of program expectations, including a description of the phase system, staff roles, and the system of rewards and sanctions. Particular emphasis should be placed on the requirements for completion of phase 1 and the development and understanding of the rules that will guide phase 2.

Based on an indepth assessment process, a comprehensive case plan will be developed prior to the youth's release from the facility. Case planning during phase 1 should not be limited to simple formulation of goals and objectives.

Instead, the implementation process must be initiated. This requirement is particularly true when identifying and securing the cooperation of those persons and agencies that will be key resources in subsequent phases (e.g., employers, community service providers). Details on case assessment and planning are provided in the case planning and management section.

Because phase 1 is designed primarily for the purposes of stabilization, assessment, and planning, individualized programming will be limited. However, generic programming should be initiated. This would include daily participation in education activities, facility-based work projects and chores, and individual and group counseling. Adherence to facility and program rules should be stressed, and the degree of compliance with those rules will be a key part of the intervention. Daily behavior, including interaction with staff and peers, should be the primary criterion upon which phase 1 rewards and sanctions are based. This should, therefore, be a primary determinant of the length of stay in this phase.

If phase 1 participants are housed in a facility where later phases of ISP activities also take place, such as day treatment, additional counseling, and educational programming, then opportunities exist. For example, if a guided group interaction (GGI) or criminal thinking errors group is part of phase 2 programming, youth could begin their participation in the group in phase 1. Similarly, assuming educational testing has been completed, youth could begin their phase 2 educational program during phase 1.

Termination. Termination from the residential phase should be contingent upon (1) the completion of assessment and case planning, (2) the meeting of the program's behavioral expectations for the phase (for example, accumulating the required points or good days), and (3) the demonstrated understanding by the youth and parents or guardians of the phase 2 requirements or expectations. The latter point is crucial. Entrance into phase 2 means the end of secure confinement and return to the community. The conditions governing the youth's freedom must be explicit, written in the form of a contract, and clearly understood and agreed upon by the youth and his or her guardians.

Phase 2. Day treatment

Purposes. In a day treatment component, youth are onsite at a facility full time during the day for educational and other programming. The goal of this phase is to allow the youth to function in a highly controlled program environment as a first step in community reintegration. This phase is characterized by a continuing emphasis on incapacitation or control—though with greater freedom than phase 1—and the initiation of intensive programming. Programming focuses on the remediation of skill deficits in areas such as education and interpersonal skills, the development of a prosocial support network, and the assumption of greater self-responsibility. The anticipated duration of this phase is 4 to 6 months.

Location. During this period the youth will live either at home, in foster care, or in a group home. For large programs, day treatment activities would take

T he goal is to allow the youth to function in a highly structured environment as a first step in community reintegration.

Y outh receive the
assistance, training,
and structure they have
often lacked.

place in an ISP center—perhaps the facility housing phase 1 youth—and could involve both phase 1 and 2 youth. In other programs, the day treatment component would be limited to phase 2 youth. In either case, program experience strongly suggests providing transportation to the day treatment center for phase 2 participants.

Programming. The control elements in this phase consist of tightly structured daytime activities of 6 hours, and house arrest, strict curfews, and a prior permission system to structure evening and weekend hours. (See figure 9 for an example of a prior permission system.)

Rehabilitative strategies during this phase focus on:

■ Educational, vocational, and social skill development.

■ Linking youth with nonprogram persons and organizations in the community.

■ Referrals for special needs, such as substance abuse or mental health counseling.

■ Working with parents to strengthen their influence and control over the youth.

■ Making preparations for phase 3 involvement in traditional school or work settings.

■ Involvement in community service or restitution programming.

■ Participation in evening and weekend recreational and cultural activities.

■ Full implementation of the system of rewards and sanctions.

Although phase 2 can be viewed as a decompression period from secure confinement, it is also one in which intense pressure is brought to bear on the juvenile in terms of extensive external control and demands for accountability. At the same time, this phase represents an opportunity for the youth to receive the individualized assistance, skills training, and structure and consistency they have often lacked.

Figure 9: Prior Permission Rules*

After earning their way off house arrest, youth will be required to enter the prior permission phase. Under prior permission, a youth must call the designated ISP counselor for permission to go from one place to another, except school, work, and program appointments. A youth cannot go to his or her next destination without the verbal permission of ISP staff. The youth will call the ISP and either speak directly with the staff, leave a message with a secretary, or leave a message on the answering machine (if after 5 p.m.). After placing the call, the youth must stay off the phone and wait until an ISP staff member returns the call. When calling for prior permission, the youth must provide the following information: time of call, name, phone number, where the youth wants to go, what time he or she wants to go, when he or she wants to return, and with whom he or she will be staying. During evening and weekend hours, on-duty staff will retrieve messages at half-hour intervals. The staff person's decision to grant or disapprove permission for the movement is final.

*Delaware County, Ohio, Intensive Supervision Manual.

While in day treatment, at least 4 hours should be spent in remedial education classes that will equip the youth to return to regular school or complete a GED. Because of the high incidence of special education needs among the target population, appropriate services should be integrated with, or provided as an adjunct to, the curriculum provided for all youth.

An additional key component in day treatment is the development of work-related skills. Each day an additional 2 to 3 hours should be spent in activities such as community service, work experience, job readiness, or world-of-work activities such as resume preparation, job search skills, or role playing of employee-employer interaction.

Finally, daytime activities should include several weekly group counseling sessions designed to deal with cognitive, behavioral, and affective issues. Several formal models of group therapy could be used, including positive peer culture, guided group interaction, or reality therapy. An alternative would be to design an eclectic approach that might include curriculum cycles focused on such topics as communication skills, values clarification, victim awareness, and criminal thinking errors. Besides these groups, an educational group format should be used to address basic life skills such as budgeting, parenting, health, and sexuality.

During the day treatment phase, all youth must be involved in other forms of programming during the evenings and weekends. Specific activities would be contingent on the youth's individualized service plan, such as the need for substance abuse treatment, but would also include elements common to all youth. Common strategies include efforts to link youth with appropriate role models and community organizations, intensive staff interactions with parents to shore up parenting authority and skills, and recreational programming. Because many clients will be drug dependent, the program should conduct random drug tests and maintain strict prohibitions against further drug involvement. All youth are also subject to phase 2 control measures, including house arrest, prior permission, and surveillance of contacts and phone calls. Finally, when the youth is functioning once again in the community, the consistent use of the reward or sanctioning system becomes very important in shaping the juvenile's behavior. Critical to this process is the ability to quickly respond to rule violations and to move youth into more controlled settings, even if for a few days. More will be said about enforcing rewards and sanctions later.

Termination. The intensive programming in phase 2 is intended to lay the groundwork for a loosening of program controls in phase 3 and a concomitant intensified reliance upon the control and resources offered by traditional social units such as the family and school. Termination from phase 2 will be contingent upon (1) having made sufficient academic or prevocational progress to warrant placement in the public schools or full-time employment; (2) having established regular involvement with one or more role models or traditional community organizations; and (3) having compiled a sufficient number of points or good days, reflecting a positive adjustment in phase 2.

The consistent use of the reward system is essential in shaping the juvenile's behavior.

Phase 3. Outreach and tracking (reintegration)

Purpose. The goal of phase 3 is to assure that the youth can function productively and responsibly in the community setting. This end is accomplished through (1) frequent client and ancillary contacts, (2) assistance to the youth and the community social units with which he or she is involved, (3) maintenance of treatment for special needs, and (4) gradual transitioning of the balance of control from the program to community institutions and ultimately to the youth. Generally, this phase can last 3 to 4 months.

Location. During phase 3 the youth lives at home or in an appropriate alternative living arrangement and goes to school or works full time. Program activities are primarily field oriented; the focus of activity will be on the youth and his or her interactions with parents, peers, school or work, and the community persons and agencies involved with the youth. If there is a centralized facility, it will likely be the location for selected activities for phase 3 youth, such as ongoing group counseling, a job preparedness curriculum, or recreational activities.

Programming. The primary phase 3 control element is that of surveillance or tracking. During this phase the youth is intensively monitored by a tracker who has a caseload of approximately 15 to 20 youth. In addition, the tracker regularly meets with family members, employers, and teachers who are familiar with the youth's progress.

Tracking coverage will be available 7 days per week and include day and evening hours. Unannounced and random contacts should be made at school or work, at home, and at other locations in the daily activities of the youth. The primary purpose of tracking should be to ensure compliance with program rules. Initially, the tracker will make multiple daily face-to-face or telephone contacts with the client. As the youth demonstrates compliance with program requirements, the number of contacts is gradually reduced.

Should the youth violate the rules of phase 3, the violation is quickly reported to the case manager. Additional control elements can be used on a case-by-case basis as sanctioning devices. These could include closer surveillance, curfews, prior permission, requirements that the youth check in periodically at the ISP facility or office, and home or short-term detention.

The tracker is primarily concerned with maintaining compliance with the conditions of liberty. The tracker reports on a weekly basis to the case manager who has worked with the youth since his or her entry into the program. The case manager continues to chart the youth's progress through a prescribed treatment plan. The tracker is accountable to the case manager to make sure that the client is achieving all agreed upon educational, work, and treatment goals.

Programming focused on rehabilitation will essentially be a continuation of those efforts begun during phase 2. However, while much of the phase 2 programming, such as education and job readiness, was delivered directly by ISP staff, responsibility for those services will likely shift to other community agencies as the youth is enrolled in school or employed. In all areas in which services are delivered by nonprogram staff, it is the responsibility of ISP staff to support the efforts of the service providers, but to also act as advocates for the youth when services are not delivered as intended or promised.

The following minimum rehabilitation strategies will be pursued in phase 3:

- Involvement with mentors or other persons serving as role models.

- Involvement with community organizations that provide recreational, cultural, or ancillary educational experiences.

- Participation in group counseling, both therapeutic and educational, as provided by ISP.

- Continuation in programs designed to address needs such as substance abuse or mental health issues.

- Intensive involvement with parents or guardians to strengthen parenting and discipline skills.

- Ongoing application of rewards and sanctions in response to daily behavior.

Highly successful models of outreach and tracking are operated by the KEY Program, Inc., and the Northeastern Family Institute, both of Massachusetts, and Youth Advocate Programs in Pennsylvania. Outreach and tracking programs are also operated by juvenile corrections agencies in Missouri, Alabama, Utah, and Maryland. The KEY Outreach and Tracking program is described in the Appendix.

Termination. The primary criterion for the termination of phase 3 is that the youth is in a position where he or she is functioning effectively without extensive ISP controls. This can be measured in terms of (1) the youth's continued involvement in school or work, (2) successful deescalation of surveillance contacts, (3) the development of bonds with prosocial peers or groups, and (4) attainment of sufficient good days or points in the reward system to meet phase 3 termination requirements.

Phase 4. Regular supervision (transition)

Purpose. The intent of phase 4 is to provide youth with the opportunity to function in the community without the benefit of the extensive controls imposed by the ISP. This is a period of testing the degree of the youth's responsibility and the strength of the support network. The goal of phase 4 is to prepare the youth for discharge from correctional supervision and to arrange for followup support services.

Location. Most aspects of the youth's case plan should be in full operation. The youth should have a stable living environment, be employed and/or completing educational objectives, and be involved with appropriate support networks.

Programming. During this phase, which might last 2 to 3 months, the youth is supervised primarily by the case manager. Supervision is generally limited to regularly scheduled meetings with the youth and family to assess progress and identify any unresolved behavioral problems. Responsibility is placed on the youth to meet the reporting obligations set forth in the phase 4 contract discussed in the case planning and management section. The structure of this phase

The intent is to provide the youth with opportunities to function effectively without extensive controls.

should be tantamount to that of regular supervision, with at least two contacts per month.

Control elements in phase 4 are minimal. While limited surveillance or curfew might be used with selected youth, the intent is for youth to rely upon internal controls and those provided by parents and others in the support network. However, all forms of control might be reimposed during this phase if slippage is apparent. In some cases, the youth may be required to return to an earlier program phase.

The services initiated in earlier phases will be continued, if appropriate. During this last supervision period, any required restitution payments should be completed and ongoing plans for needed substance abuse counseling should be finalized. The youth must continue to remain law abiding and drug free (random drug testing may be used as necessary). Particular attention should be paid to maintaining the youth's involvement with prosocial forces in the community, ensuring disengagement from delinquent peers, and continuing the support of parents, teachers, and employers.

During the transition phase, the case manager should ensure that the youth is involved with a support network that can continue to provide a high level of emotional support for the client. A strongly recommended option for providing ongoing support and encouragement is the recruitment of a mentor. The mentor, who might be a college student or an adult from the youth's community, should continue to work with the youth after the youth is terminated from supervision. The intent is to provide a bridge for the youth, in terms of support and consistency, between the program and unsupervised community living. This bridging is critical because it is a common experience with ISP's that youth begin to act out shortly before or immediately after program termination. In the future, volunteer mentors, who work one-on-one with troubled youth, will be a significant feature of correctional programs.

Phase 5. Discharge and followup

The youth should be formally discharged from correctional supervision when he or she has completed the regular supervision component and a community-based support system is in place. Agreements should be reached with the mentor to continue the relationship with the youth for a minimum of 2 months. At the point of discharge, the case manager certifies that the client has completed all goals established in the case plan. The case manager also notifies the local juvenile justice official of the youth's accomplishments. This feedback is important in winning continued support for the intensive supervision program.

Program termination should be noted with a small ceremony that recognizes the hard work of the youths and their families. The case manager should be available to the client for occasional informal advice and counseling. Followup should include occasional contact with the youth initiated by the case manager.

The phase system described in this section is designed to allow a youth to gradually progress from total program control to self-control. The structure of the phases allows for rehabilitation to occur through the program and service components that are described in the next section.

Program components

This chapter describes the central components of the ISP model, including case planning and management, program rewards and sanctions, and program services. These components operate throughout the program phases. For each of these components, basic policies and rationales are provided, followed by a discussion of the way in which policy might be translated into practice.

Case planning and management

Policies

The following policies should guide the case management process:

1. Case assessment and a written case plan will be completed for each participant within the first 30 days of program acceptance and prior to termination of phase 1. Assessments should include structured risk and needs assessments, the results of previous and current clinical and educational evaluations, detailed examination of the circumstances surrounding the current and prior offenses, and an identification of youth and family strengths.

2. Case plans must reflect the underlying theory of delinquency causation and the specific risk factors associated with each youth. The case plan should identify intervention priorities, including long range goals and intermediate objectives.

3. A behavioral contract based on the case plan should be developed for each phase.

4. A formal reassessment process should be conducted each 60 to 90 days during Phases 2 through 4. The reassessment should be based on the youth's progress in meeting objectives, compliance with program regulations, newly identified needs, and the youth's community behavior during the most recent supervision period.

5. The primary responsibility for case management should rest with one ISP staff person (case manager) who should retain responsibility for the case through all five phases. The case manager is responsible for case assessment and planning, referral and monitoring of service delivery, and reassessment. Case managers should have caseloads no larger than 15–20 clients.

Rationale. The rationale for these case management policies derives both from actual program experience and from the theoretical assumptions underlying the intervention. Experience indicates that continuous case management is necessary to assure that services are coordinated and that there is accountability in the service delivery process. Theory suggests that the case manager may be a key role model and an integral part of the youth's support network. Frequent changes in this role or lack of clarity as to who has responsibility will likely prevent relationship development and may introduce additional instability and uncertainty into the offender's life.

T he case manager should be a role model and an integral part of the support network.

The need for a comprehensive case assessment and development of a multipronged intervention strategy is dictated by the many factors associated with the cause of delinquency. Although theory indicates the fundamental components of causation (and therefore basic strategies), it also recognizes that a variety of circumstances influence behavior at the individual level. This supports the need for individualized assessment and planning that takes into account specific, as opposed to aggregate, risk factors. Further, the philosophy of risk control, as well as resource constraints, demands that the ISP not attempt to address all youth problems. Instead, those risk and need factors that are most closely tied to the possibility of reoffending need to be targeted.

The contracting requirements derive primarily from learning theory. When youth know what is expected from them at each step of the process, there is a greater likelihood that objectives will be attained. Further, the specification and application of rewards and sanctions is fundamental both to motivation and reinforcement. Finally, given the volatile nature of the youth's behavior and circumstances, regular reassessments are necessary to ensure the relevance of the intervention plan.

Case assessment

The assessment process must address those factors that are closely related to the youth's risk of reoffending. Many of these factors will have been previously identified because the risk and needs will have been used in the process of screening youth for program eligibility.

The development of an effective intervention strategy will likely require a much more indepth assessment. For example, while an initial risk and needs screening may indicate a history of mental health or substance abuse problems, it may be necessary to arrange formal evaluation to determine the status and nature of such problems. Although risk assessment instruments are useful in identifying the likelihood of recidivism, they are based on aggregate measures. It is imperative, therefore, that assessment consider the history, characteristics, and circumstances of each youth. In doing so, the traditional dimensions should be explored, such as family history and functioning, peers, substance abuse, etc., along with factors that are frequently overlooked. For example, research has consistently demonstrated the influence on recidivism of factors such as sexual and physical abuse, special education, and the presence of developmental disabilities. In addition, juvenile agency staff tend to focus on offender needs and ignore the characteristics of the juveniles' offenses. Detailed exploration of the circumstances, including cognitive processes or affective states, surrounding the youth's offenses often reveal key motivations or triggers to youth behavior.

The assessment should also take into account youth, family, peer, and community strengths. Although high-risk youth typically experience multiple deficits, characteristics and relationships also exist that can be used as stepping stones for developing a nondelinquent lifestyle. Such strengths may be limited and appear insignificant, such as a good relationship with the basketball coach and a quick wit, but should not be discounted in the planning stages.

Strategies for juvenile supervision

A promising case planning tool is the Strategies for Juvenile Supervision (SJS) system (Krahn, Arling, and Lerner, 1988). SJS was developed to provide a structured, quick way to evaluate juvenile offenders and to develop supervision strategies based on offender types. Youth entering ISP may be labeled serious juvenile offenders, yet they may differ considerably in living stability, acceptance of criminal behavior, emotional needs, educational level, and other factors. ISP workers require both understanding of the individual and flexibility in applying different supervisory techniques to deal effectively with a variety of juveniles and their problems. Staff need to know when to confront or support, be directive, trust, or recommend treatment. Those who rely too heavily on one method—who are, for example, always domineering, tend to work effectively with some offenders and not others. Staff who apply a range of supervisory techniques can be more effective with a greater number of offenders.

Under the SJS system, a 50-minute structured offender interview is used to assess major areas in a juvenile's life that contribute to delinquency. This includes offense patterns, school, family, interpersonal relationships, substance use, current problems, and future plans. The assessment evaluates factual information as well as the juvenile's attitudes and emotional responses. Interview responses are scored to classify juveniles in one of four groupings: Selective Intervention, Casework/Control, Environmental Structure, and Limit Setting. Once classified, supervision and case planning guides help structure case plans and supervision strategies for each offender type.

SJS addresses the qualitative aspects of juvenile supervision by suggesting specific strategies that are most likely to result in positive change on the part of the juvenile offender. The SJS Supervision Guide provides specific recommendations as to which of the qualitatively different supervision approaches will be most effective with a particular juvenile. For example, some juveniles may respond most positively to a counseling or problem-solving approach, while others may respond to clear statements of behavioral expectations and strict enforcement of sanctions.

SJS has a threefold purpose:

1. It provides the caseworker with a set of predictions about the juvenile's likely response to supervision.

2. It provides an immediate consult or second opinion for understanding case dynamics and formulating supervision strategy.

3. It allows the caseworker to assume a proactive rather than reactive stance in the supervision process.

Selective intervention. Juveniles in the Selective Intervention (SI) group are characterized by a generally prosocial value structure and stable lifestyle. The offense history is usually limited; the current offense is often the first. The offenders get into trouble because of a core emotional problem or a significant change in personal or family status which disrupts normal functioning. They

S taff must be flexible in applying supervisory techniques.

often present specific problems, such as sex offending or substance abuse, which are likely to continue without intervention and treatment. Although they are frequently able to function vocationally and interpersonally, the likelihood of continued criminal involvement is great unless treatment needs are handled appropriately.

Under supervision, these juveniles tend to present the fewest problems and require the least amount of time. These juveniles tend to make good use of intensive individual or family counseling and usually are found to be honest and reliable in their reporting.

Casework/control. The Casework/Control (CC) group is characterized by chronic and generalized instability and a variety of problems. Although these juveniles often have average intelligence and possess reasonable vocational skills, their instability may be manifested in substance abuse, serious emotional problems, frequent changes in residence, and attachment to others who are equally unstable. They come from chaotic family backgrounds, and a great deal of family support should not be expected.

Criminal behavior in the CC group ranges from the trivial to the serious and seems to reflect their lack of direction. These juveniles have difficulty generating or maintaining a commitment to any program of change. Generally, CC is a difficult group to supervise. Case activity is high with this multineed group, and crisis situations can be frequent.

Environmental structure. The Environmental Structure (ES) group is characterized by a lack of social and vocational skills. These individuals often have intellectual deficits, are often easily led by delinquent peers, and lack the judgment to know when they are being exploited. Involvement in crime is impulsive, unsophisticated, and frequently motivated by a desire for others' acceptance. Although their behavior can be dangerous and assaultive, their motivation is seldom malicious.

Supervision for the ES group should include the development of survival skills, improved social skills, and increased impulse control. The dependency noted in this group can be used to advantage during the course of supervision. ES juveniles are often eager to please and will frequently respond to supportive and nonthreatening guidance.

Limit setting. The Limit Setting (LS) group is best characterized by a criminal orientation and a general lack of commitment to prosocial values. Although they tend to have sound social skills, the criminal behavior within this group is generally motivated by money, excitement, and power. Criminal histories are often lengthy and marked by numerous felonies and violent or aggressive offenses.

Treatment is generally rejected by the juvenile except as a means to avoid more restrictive sanctions. Supervision must focus responsibility on the offender, stress accountability, and must provide control and surveillance when appropriate. Limits and consequences for misbehavior must be detailed in advance and all rules enforced consistently. Where possible, attempts should be made to foster an interest in legal means to meet the need for money, power, and excitement. The goal is to modify a value system that is at odds with accepted norms.

Case planning

Once a juvenile is assigned to an SJS strategy, the caseworker is able to use the information gathered in the SJS interview and the predictions contained in the Supervision Guide to prepare an individualized case plan. The case plan is critical in that it allows the caseworker to focus resources on critical problem areas and to influence case outcomes rather than simply react to emergencies.

The SJS case planning system is a problem-solving model that uses analysis of juvenile weaknesses and strengths as found in Clear's (n.d.) Objectives-Based Case Planning document. Based on Lewin's force-field analysis, this tool provides a systematic technique for identifying and prioritizing the importance of individual risk factors and those factors that are conducive to law-abiding behavior. The case planning process consists of the following components:

1. Analysis:
   – Identification of problems.
   – Identification of strengths and resources.

2. Problem prioritization.

3. Writing the plan.

4. Monitoring and updating (reassessment).

Analysis includes the SJS interview, the risk/needs assessments, and all other methods that the caseworker uses to obtain information about the juvenile offender. In many cases, the assessment results in an extensive list of problem areas and a relatively short list of strengths and resources. Figure 10 provides an example of a full listing (without prioritization) of an offender's strengths (driving forces) and risk factors (forces restraining law-abiding behavior).

The case plan should build on the youth's strengths and target for intervention those risk and need factors that are most clearly related to the likelihood of reoffending. Through a systematic problem prioritization, the caseworker is able to reduce a lengthy list of problem areas to a more manageable few. Problem prioritization is a key step in the process in that it assists the caseworker in selecting the key problems which, if solved, may reduce the likelihood of further delinquency. This implies a focus on risk control, rather than addressing all the youth's needs. Problem prioritization involves the following considerations:

T he case plan should build on the youth's strengths and target the factors that increase the likelihood of reoffending.

Figure 10: Force Field On Probationer Henry Ward

Forces Driving More Law-Abiding Behavior	Law-Abiding Behavior	Forces Restraining Law-Abiding Behavior
1. Length of time since last serious offense (4 years)	-------- > < --------	1. Very quick temper
2. Strong relationship with mother	-------- > < --------	2. Previous inability to successfully complete probation without violations
3. No serious mental or emotional problems	-------- > < --------	3. Friendship includes persons who are marginally deviant
4. Has been able to find several jobs on his own	-------- > < --------	4. Seriousness of current offense
5. Apparently wants to work as a truck driver	-------- > < --------	5. Transient background
6. High-average intelligence	-------- > < --------	6. Lack of male role model
7. School seems to be a possibility	-------- > < --------	7. Immature behavior patterns
8. Newly developed relationship with Fr. Brown	-------- > < --------	8. Lack of self-understanding
9. Apparently developing religious ties	-------- > < --------	9. Poor school history
10. Apparent previous cooperative attitude on probation	-------- > < --------	10. Mother apparently supports some antisocial behavior
11. Generally good physical health	-------- > < --------	11. Sporadic work record
12. Girlfriend's parents' strong disapproval of the relationship	-------- > < --------	12. Unwillingness to face the "realities" of his offense
	< --------	13. Expresses antisocial attitudes
	< --------	14. Occasional abuse of drugs and alcohol
	< --------	15. Presence of "steady" girlfriend
	< --------	16. Aimless use of free time

1. Review of problem strength: An analysis of the importance of a given problem in generating further delinquency.

2. Review of problem alterability: The caseworker must determine the degree to which a problem situation can be altered or the degree of resistance which might be encountered in attempting to alter the situation. For example, ISP is highly unlikely to have any impact on the extent of social disorganization in a neighborhood. However, it may well be able to identify a role model for the youth to overcome the effects of social disorganization.

3. Speed of solution: The caseworker must weigh the time needed to solve a problem and the additional resources that might be required to effect change.

4. Problem interdependence: Multiproblem cases must be reviewed for causal relationships among the various problem areas. By selecting root problems for specific attention, the caseworker is able to focus on those few key problems which, if solved, may have positive results in other problem areas.

By applying the problem prioritization steps, the caseworker is able to select those most appropriate for immediate attention. Each of these is addressed in a Written Case Plan which includes the following components.

Problem statement: A statement of the juvenile's problem areas.

Long-range goal: A statement of the juvenile's behavior when the problem is solved.

Short-range objectives: A statement and timeframe of the behaviors that the juvenile will complete to achieve the long-range goal.

Action plan: The step-by-step detail by which each short-range objective will be completed. The Action Plan includes expectations for the juvenile, the caseworker, and any others who are actively involved in the case plan.

Responsibilities/resources: A description of who is responsible and the resources available for assisting the juvenile to meet his or her objectives.

The case plan should clearly state the goals, the intermediate steps toward those goals, the resources to be used in achieving them, and the target dates for completion. The case plan should set achievable objectives for the youth in all relevant areas. Objectives should be measurable; that is, they should be specific and stated in behavioral terms to determine whether or not they have been met. They should also be realistic to avoid setting up the youth for repeat cycles of failure.

One example of an objectives-based case plan is provided in figure 11. Note that the objectives are stated in terms of the expected outcome behaviors for the youth and are clearly measurable. Objectives should not focus on what ISP staff will be doing, but on what the youth will accomplish. For example, "John will enroll in GED classes at Roxbury H.S. by 10/1/90," is more appropriate than, "counselor will refer youth for GED."

Objectives-based contracting

A behavioral contract based on the case plan should be developed for each phase. The contract should (1) reflect the relationship between the objectives for each phase and the long-range goals, (2) be written in specific behavioral terms; (3) be developed in conjunction with the youth and parents, (4) specify the rewards and sanctions associated with compliance or noncompliance with the contract, and (5) have attached to it a copy of the generic rules and requirements that apply to the appropriate phase.

The rewards and consequences for meeting or not meeting contract objectives should also be specified. Typically, the reward for doing well on probation is limited to the sometimes distant possibility of getting off. However, the need for consistent reinforcement suggests that rewards and consequences should be more tangible and immediate, such as lifting or imposing a curfew or revoking or giving back a driver's license.

The rewards and consequences for meeting objectives should be tangible and immediate.

T he involvement of youth, parents, and service providers in the development of the behavioral contract is critical.

Figure 11: Sample Case Planning Format

Client:	JJ
Phase:	2
Date:	8/1/91

Area: Family

Goals: To return home by 10/1 and remain in home with minimal conflict with mother.

Phase Objectives:
1. To achieve prerelease status at group home by 9/1 and release by 10/1.
2. To complete all chores and adhere to 7 p.m. curfew while on weekend passes at home during September.
3. To not argue with mother about restrictions on peers in the home.
4. To attend all family counseling sessions in September and October.

Steps: N/A

Responsibilities: CM complete court papers for release from group home.
Mother attend family counseling and ISP parents' group.

Resources: Group home and ISP staff, Mr. Johnson at Lighthouse Center, CM.

Area: Education/Work

Goals: To get GED and enroll in vocational school by end of phase 4.

Phase Objectives:
1. To complete remedial work in math and reading and pass tests at ISP school by 10/1.
2. To complete GED prep work at Roxbury H.S. by 2/15/92 (test on 3/2/92).
3. To obtain brochures and applications for vocational schools by 11/1.

Steps: Continue with tutor; enroll in GED at Roxbury; clarify vocational interests.

Responsibilities: CM identify area vocational schools and sources of scholarships or other funding. Tutor available three times per week next 2 months.

Resources: Tutor, Mrs. White at Roxbury, Joint Area Vocational, Electronics Academy, ISP school staff.

Area: Peers

Goals: Disengage from McGruder St. crowd.

Phase Objectives:
1. To have no contact with Ray B., Raheem, and Rabbit on weekend passes and after return home.
2. Finish work on "easily influenced" problem in group.
3. Once home, meet with mentor three times per week.
4. Complete scuba course or weightlifting program at YMCA.

Steps: N/A

Responsibilities: Mentor available three times per week; mother and surveillance staff monitor friends.

Resources: Mentor, ISP group, YMCA.

The meaningful involvement of youth, parents, and service providers in the development of the behavioral contract is critical to the case plan's success. First, the unilateral imposition of goals and objectives may result in specification of outcomes that have little relevance or meaning to the youth. Without a sense of ownership, these goals are not likely to be attained. Second, a goal-setting process that excludes the youth and family may reinforce perceptions of powerlessness. It will also result in missed opportunities for both the youth and family to develop skills in what may well be an area of considerable weakness. Third, if parties external to the ISP unit, such as parents, school staff, and mentors, are to be used as coimplementors of the intervention strategy, they should also serve as coauthors of that strategy. Their involvement will not only facilitate buy-in, but help assure a coordinated approach.

Reassessment

In practice, the nature of intensive supervision is such that cases will be reassessed on a weekly and in some cases a daily basis. These will result in ongoing informal adjustments to the case plan. However, periodic formal reassessments should be conducted and documented. At a minimum, the development of an updated plan and new contract for each phase requires that a formal reassessment occur at these intervals. However, reassessment should also occur at prescribed intervals (e.g., every 60 days) within each phase.

If case plans are to be meaningful, they must be viewed as dynamic, flexible, and responsive. Consequently, reassessments should take into account changes in the youth, his or her environment, and available resources, including the quality of service provided by currently used resources. The reassessment process should also incorporate a critical review of the continuing appropriateness of identified goals and objectives. Greater knowledge of the youth and his or her changes, may result in modifying or abandoning previously selected strategies. As part of the reassessment process, the use of risk and need reassessment instruments can provide an objective perspective on case progress. They quantify and document changes in the level of risk and need presented by each youth. Figure 12 provides an example of a structured risk reassessment instrument, developed for the Michigan Office of Children and Youth Services (OCYS). Note that the first four items on the reassessment scale are the same as those found in figure 4.

Program rewards and sanctions

Policy

A comprehensive system of rewards and sanctions must be implemented to reinforce achievements, hold youth accountable for program and community violations, and shape everyday behaviors.

Rationale for policy. Just as delinquent behavior is learned and supported by the acceptance and reinforcement of the negative peer group, so too must it be reduced by the continuous positive reinforcements of the legitimate social units working with the youth.

Operational strategy

The system of rewards and sanctions is crucial in all facets of the ISP intervention. Not only ISP staff, but other key actors in the youth's intervention, such as parents and teachers, should consistently reinforce positive and negative behaviors.

Reassessment should incorporate a critical review of the continuing appropriateness of goals and objectives.

Figure 12: Michigan Youth Services Risk Reassessment: Scale Community Supervision

Rate items 1–4 the same as the numbered items on the initial risk assessment scale.   **Score**

1. Age at first adjudication   _____
   11 or under 3
   12–14 2
   15 1
   16 or over 0

2. Number of prior arrests   _____
   None 0
   One or two 1
   Three or more 2

3. Current offense   _____
   Nonassaultive offense (i.e., property, drug, etc.) 2
   All others 0

4. Number of prior out-of-home placements   _____
   One or fewer 0
   Two or more 1

Rate the remaining items based on behavior over the last 3 months.

5. Current school status   _____
   Attending regularly, occasional truancy only,
      or graduated/GED 0
   Dropped out of school 1
   Expelled, suspended, or habitually truant 2

6. Current drug or alcohol use   _____
   No known use 0
   Occasional use, some disruption of functioning 2
   Frequent use, serious disruption of functioning 4

7. Level of parental or caretaker control   _____
   Generally effective 0
   Inconsistent and/or ineffective 1
   Little or no supervision provided 2

8. Peer relationships   _____
   Good support and influence; associates with
      nondelinquent friends 0
   Not peer-oriented or some companions with
      delinquent orientations 2
   Most companions are delinquent or involved in gangs 4

                                                               Total Score: _____

Risk Assessment
   0–8   Low risk
   9–13   Moderate risk
   14–20   High risk

The reinforcement system has two dimensions. One focuses on the rewards associated with the attainment of contract objectives and the sanctions associated with significant program violations. The other is concerned with responding to day-to-day noncompliance with program requirements and community expectations. In each dimension, sanctions should be:

■ Clearly identified before they are applied.

- Applied in a timely fashion.

- Tailored to each youth to maximize their meaningfulness.

- Consist in their application.

- Proportionate to the magnitude of the event.

Rewards. Youth should receive positive reinforcements when they attain long- and short-term objectives. Although the attainment of some goals may carry intrinsic rewards—a job, for instance, leads to regular income—youth need additional reinforcement through strong social approval and support of the accomplishment. Consequently, achievement of primary objectives, such as the GED, should be recognized through special benefits such as trips to entertainment and sports events, special recreational opportunities such as camping or ski trips, or special ceremonies with extensive family and community involvement. Similar reinforcements might also be applied as youth graduate from one program phase to the next.

Small gains should also be positively reinforced. Accomplishments that might be taken for granted with other youth, such as going to school every day for a week, may deserve special attention among high-risk populations. By reinforcing this particular step, the likelihood of the youth taking the next step—going to school for 2 weeks straight—is enhanced. Rewards for such accomplishments might include awarding additional program credit days, giving extra points or coupons that can be used to purchase special privileges (for example, a day spent without prior permission rules or a dinner at a favorite restaurant).

Although the variety of rewards is limited only by staff creativity, care should be taken to select a reward that is meaningful to the youth while retaining a sense of proportion both in relation to the accomplishment and in relation to the rewards received by other program youth for similar accomplishments.

Persons other than program staff must also reinforce accomplishments. ISP should work with parents, mentors, teachers, and others in the youth's support network to assure that they too are sensitive to gains and that they provide their own forms of recognition.

Sanctions. ISP must pay careful attention to providing effective sanctions for negative behavior. The nature of the program's response to rules violations or behaviors that are clearly associated with the risk of reoffending, such as substance abuse, will heavily influence youth progress and perceptions of program integrity.

As with the reward system, potential sanctions should be clearly identified in advance and applied in a consistent and timely fashion. Perhaps most importantly, sanctions should be tied to the severity of the infraction. Given the highly structured nature of the program, numerous technical violations are likely to surface that would normally go undetected. Under such conditions, an immediate resort to revocation of probation would be unfair to the youth and

> **E**ffective sanctions will influence perceptions of program integrity.

The case manager should have the authority to enforce short-term detention when necessary.

defeat the program. In response to these concerns, several intensive programs have developed explicit and progressive sanctioning schedules. An example is provided in figure 13.

Sanctions may include temporary loss of program privileges, reimposition of more intrusive controls, and more restrictive curfew for less serious violations. Moderate level sanctions might include imposition of multiple control elements, such as house arrest combined with increased surveillance, or the assignment of additional community service hours. Short-term detention up to 7 days should be an available sanction, but should be reserved for those who are chronic violators of program rules, those who repeatedly refuse to comply with lesser sanctions, and those whose infractions are serious. The case manager should have the capability and authority to quickly enforce short-term detention when necessary. However, all detention decisions should be reviewed by the program administration.

Figure 13: Violation Categories and Appropriate Sanctions (example)

Category 1 Violations	Category 2 Violations	Category 3 Violations
Curfew hours	Chronic repetition of Category 1 violations	Conviction on multiple misdemeanors
AWOL < 24 hours	AWOL > 24 hours	Conviction on felony
Truancy	Abuse of alcohol or drugs	Beyond control of program staff
Failure to report	Fired from job	Active participation in gang activities
Incomplete chores	Refuse to attend court-ordered program	Chronic repetition of Category 2 violations
Associate w/negative peer	Abusive behavior or assault in program	
In off-limits area	Carry weapon	
Fail to pay restitution	New arrest for misdemeanor or felony	
Other	Other	

Category 1 Sanctions	Category 2 Sanctions	Category 3 Sanctions
Reprimand	Category 1 sanction and/or:	Cat. 1,2 sanctions and/or:
Stricter curfew	Extended house arrest	7-day detention
Loss of privilege(s)	Increased urinalysis	Electronic surveillance
Loss of days	Admin. review hearing	Return to phase 1
Increased surveillance	Weekend detention	Revoke to inpatient
Short-term house arrest	Court review/admonish	Revoke to institution
Add community service hrs.	Return to earlier phase	
Other proportional	Other proportional	

Termination from the ISP should be pursued only with those youth for whom all possible inprogram sanctions have been exhausted and with youth who have committed new felony offenses. Unsuccessful program terminations resulting from chronic or serious infractions will result in placement in a secure correctional facility. For those youth terminated unsuccessfully due to chronic problems such as substance abuse or mental health needs, residential treatment settings would be a preferred post-ISP placement option.

Responding to daily behavior. The extensive interaction between staff and youth in an ISP provides the opportunity to observe the behavior of youth on a daily basis. The implementation of a system of sanctions and rewards tied to daily behavior provides a mechanism for shaping those behaviors.

Systems designed to reinforce youth behavior at the daily level use some variation of a token economy. Points, tokens, credits, or other units are added or deleted from the youth's account to reflect the degree of compliance with expected behaviors. Accumulation of the requisite number of points governs movement through different program levels or phases. The incentive to move to a new level is greater privileges and freedom.

A frequently used variation of this approach focuses on the withholding or rewarding of credit days in response to behavior in the program, at home and school, and in the community. The rules governing behavior in each of these areas are defined and detailed as part of the youth's contract for each of the program's phases. For example, the rules may require that the youth attend all classes, be on time, and exhibit appropriate behavior in all classes. This requirement will be monitored through the use of a school report on which teachers grade the youth's behavior daily. An example of a daily school report used in Lucas County, Ohio, can be found in figure 14.

Rules typically also specify expectations for the home, such as curfew and chores, and in the community, such as restrictions on peers. Compliance with these rules is also monitored daily through the activities of surveillance officers, contacts with parents, and self-reporting. The judgment as to whether the youth should be awarded a credit day is made daily and is contingent on the youth's compliance with all conditions. Consequently, reinforcement is behavior-specific and occurs almost immediately.

The rewards and sanctions in this approach are related to restrictions on movement and the extent of control to which the youth is subjected. When participants earn sufficient credit days to move to a new phase, they are rewarded with such things as the lifting of house arrest, relaxed curfews, and reduced reporting requirements. Negative consequences associated with bad days include lack of progress toward termination and the maintenance of current levels of control. Significant compliance or noncompliance can result in qualitatively different reinforcements such as special privileges (e.g., the awarding of bonus days) or restrictions (e.g., return to an earlier phase).

Compliance or noncompliance can result in qualitatively different reinforcements.

Participation in positive social activities reinforces the youth's commitment to conventional values.

Intensive Supervision Unit — Daily School Report

For: _____   Date: _____

Day: _____

Subject	Teacher's Signature	Completed Assignments	Classroom Behavior	Comments

+ = No problem
- = Not acceptable/problem

COMMENTS — If there is a problem for the day/period, please indicate the problem involved. Additional input is welcomed, positive or negative.

Call _____, Ext. _____, to reach _____.

Program services

Overview

The program model consists of a mix of supervision and services designed to address those risk factors that contribute to the development or continuation of delinquent behavior. Service delivery is guided by the philosophy of risk control, which incorporates both incapacitative and rehabilitative strategies. Offender accountability is also stressed.

Program services should be shaped by the assumptions of Integrated Social Control theory. Consequently, intervention should focus on (1) developing youth bonds to conventional values, activities, persons, and institutions; (2) providing youth with the personal, social, and technical skills to function in conventional society; (3) providing access to meaningful opportunities to exercise those skills; and (4) reducing the influence of delinquent peers as a socializing force. Delinquency research has consistently shown that participation in positive social activities, such as attending school, possessing a job, or belonging to community groups reinforces the youth's commitment to conventional values. The development of prosocial values and behaviors shapes the youth's internal controls against recidivism as the external controls provided by ISP are gradually reduced.

Direct vs. brokered services

A single agency cannot offer the full range of services required by this program design. The mix of direct versus brokered services will vary based on local resources. Some organizations, for example, may have the inhouse capability of providing substance abuse treatment or formal family therapy, while other agencies will need to rely on local service providers for these resources. There is no presumption that either directly provided or brokered services are preferable. Whatever the mix, the need for comprehensive services makes effective community linkages a critical program consideration. The section on Context and implementation provides more detail about forging effective program linkages.

Service areas

High-risk youth are typically multiproblem offenders. Case planning and service delivery must be able to identify and access resources to address the range of offender needs that are most closely related to the individual's likelihood of reoffending. Researchers expect all program youth to require some common services—these are identified as core services. In addition, it is likely that each offender will have specialized needs in one or more areas. Services addressing those needs are referred to as supportive. The following pages highlight and provide examples for potential services in each area.

Core Service Areas

- Supervision and control.
- Individual/group counseling.
- Family interventions.
- Peer groups.
- Education.
- Job training/employment.
- Community service/restitution.
- Substance abuse.
- Recreation/leisure/cultural.

Supportive Service Areas

- Residential living.
- Medical/health.
- Mental health.
- Special education.
- Special needs offenders.

Core services

Supervision and control. This consists of activities designed to provide external constraints of the youth's behavior, monitor that behavior, and strengthen the youth's adherence to and acceptance of the rules of the program and the larger society. As reflected in the phase system, services in this area are most intensive in the initial program stages and are progressively reduced as the youth develops greater internal controls. Specific program elements in this area include:

- Secure custody in phase 1.
- Complete structuring of the youth's day in phase 2 and the initial months of phase 3.

Supervision and control are reduced as the youth develops greater internal controls.

- 16 hours per day/7 days per week surveillance coverage in phases 2 and 3, which is intended to ensure compliance with program rules for home, school and work, and community living.

- The use of restrictive curfews, house arrest, and prior permission in phase 2 and in subsequent program phases as warranted by offender behavior.

- Frequent and unannounced urinalysis where substance abuse is an issue.

- The optional use of electronic surveillance in selected cases.

- Staff on call 24 hours a day, 7 days a week.

- Daily sanctions for inappropriate behavior.

- Intensive contact with the case manager for purposes of counseling and monitoring.

- Ongoing coordination with parents, mentors, service providers, and supervision and services.

- The ability to move youth between levels of restrictiveness (to an earlier program phase or short-term detention).

Figure 15 provides an illustration of the way in which supervision and control strategies might be put into operation.

Individual and group counseling. Informal counseling, which is continuously provided by all program staff and focused on day-to-day adjustment issues, is crucial in developing relationships between youth and staff. However, ISP's should also involve youth in a program of formal counseling, either individually or as part of a group. A variety of counseling techniques and intervention strategies are available, including Reality Therapy, Client-Centered Counseling, Positive Peer Culture, and Rational-Emotive Therapy. Typically, these modalities have a psychotherapeutic or behavior modification thrust. Such an approach should be complemented by an emphasis on the development of enhanced competency in everyday living, focusing on skills such as problem solving and decisionmaking, goal setting, and communication. Further, skill-oriented counseling can treat specific issues that are useful to the high-risk youth, such as dealing with peer pressure, youth and teacher or employer conflict, job search and interviewing strategies, and money management.

The Lucas County, Ohio, Intensive Supervision Unit is one example of an intensive program that uses both therapeutic and skill-development counseling approaches. Youth with particularly problematic family relationships are involved in Structural Family Therapy, a formal model designed to identify and address the roots of family dysfunction.

A credentialed therapist conducts weekly sessions. At the same time, a less formal weekly group that focuses on life skills is held for all intensive youth. The intensive unit case managers conduct these sessions that also involve community resource persons. The group uses both educational and experiential activities that focus on topics such as use of community resources, family planning, parental relationships, health (including drug use), and vocational possibilities.

Figure 15: Supervision—Control Components by Phase

Component	Phase 1 Residential	Phase 2 Day Treatment	Phase 3 Outreach and Tracking	Phase 4 Transition	Phase 5 Discharge and Followup
Secure Care	Up to 45 days	Short-term detention or return to ISP facility as required for program violations			N/A
Day Structuring	N/A	Duration of Phase 4–6 months	Duration of Phase 3–4 months	As needed	N/A
Surveillance	N/A	3–4 times daily, months 1 and 2; 1–2 times daily, months 3 to end.	2–3 times daily, month 1; 1–2 times daily month 2; 1–2 times weekly, months 3 to end.	1 time weekly, month 1; as needed, months 2 to end.	N/A
House Arrest	N/A	Total, month 1; partial, month 2; as needed, months 3 to end.	As needed for program violations		N/A
Prior Permission	N/A	Required, month 2; as needed, months 3 to end.	As needed for program violations		N/A
Curfew	N/A	Months 2–6 with decreasing restrictiveness.	Required, months 1 and 2; as needed, months 3 to end	As needed	N/A
Daily Sanctioning	By program staff	By program staff	By program staff and parents	By parents	By parents
Case Manager Contacts	3–5 times weekly	3–5 times weekly, months 1–2; 2 + times weekly, months 3 to end (includes weekend coverage).	1–2 times weekly, months 1–2; 1 time weekly, months 3 to end.	2 times monthly	Sporadic or as requested by youth
Urinalysis	N/A	Random 2 times per week	Random 1 time per week	Random	N/A
Electronic Surveillance	N/A	As needed—selected cases			N/A

Family interventions. Because the family is the primary unit of socialization, yet is frequently a source of dysfunction for juvenile offenders, programming must incorporate family intervention strategies. In this service area, the family, especially the parents, is the target of intervention, and not the youth alone.

Family-based interventions may also incorporate many formal and informal techniques. Formal family therapy, parent support groups, and intensive family interventions, such as the Homebuilders model, are all options for ISP. An additional promising approach is the use of trained family advocates who work as part of the ISP team and who provide multiweekly home-based services. Services include informal family counseling, skill and communication development, and basic assistance in areas such as budgeting, nutrition, and access to community resources.

Finally, a number of ISP's are making concentrated efforts to work with parents to improve their discipline skills. These efforts usually focus on the use of the ISP reward and sanction system. The intent is to convince parents of the need for consistent reinforcement, to get them to support ISP staff in these sanctions, and to assist parents in developing their own skills. Many programs specifically

Programs should incorporate strategies for dysfunctional families.

Services to increase the educational skills of high-risk youth are critical.

identify the objective of transferring the program's focus of control to the parents.

Peer groups. While involvement with delinquent peers is a key to understanding the causes of delinquency, developing interventions focused on the peer group have been problematic at best. While some success has been achieved with Guided Group Interaction or Positive Peer Culture models in residential settings, these have not transferred well to community-based settings. Experimentation with the use of paraprofessional street workers to influence delinquent peer group activities—usually in relation to gangs—has produced marginal results.

Because it is difficult to impact directly the delinquent peer group, the approaches that are used must be designed to provide juveniles with the desire and skills to disengage themselves from negative peers. Such strategies include counseling that focuses on peer pressure, values clarification, and goal identification. The impact of counseling on these issues can be enhanced via the group setting, where commonality of adolescent experience can be recognized, solutions jointly developed, and progress mutually supported. At the same time, efforts must also be made to disconnect youth from delinquent peers by providing opportunities for interaction with conventional peers and activities.

Education. Services designed to increase the educational skills of high-risk youth are critical if their stakes in conformity are to be raised. School failure plays a central role in weakening self-concept, which induces a sense of strain and blocks opportunities for success.

The link between educational deficits and delinquency is a primary rationale for the emphasis on alternative and remedial education in phase 2 of the ISP model. The goals of this phase are to prepare the youth to obtain high school credentials (GED), or to elevate skills to the point that the youth can return to school at or near an age-appropriate grade level.

Research has shown that remedial education efforts with delinquent populations can be successful when (1) an individualized approach to assessment and programming is used, (2) nontraditional materials and methods such as computer technology are used, (3) academic efforts offer a high degree of supervision and support (for example, low student-teacher ratios and teachers with extensive experience with, and empathy for, high-risk populations), and (4) careful transition and followup support when the youth has returned to a regular school setting.

The transition from an essentially sheltered environment to the open public school setting is highly problematic. First, youth are not likely to be welcomed back by teachers and administrators who have previously had negative experiences with them. This reaction will require efforts to enlist the cooperation of school staff and to provide these staff with ongoing support. Many ISP's have stressed the need for close cooperation with schools and have been able to provide the desired support by immediately sanctioning school violations and by daily or weekly contacts with teachers and administrators. Second, the youth will require ongoing support to maintain academic progress, develop self-discipline, and deal with peers. This support can be provided by linking youth with tutors or mentors, allowing them access to the resources of the day treatment center, and continuing their involvement with the individual and group counseling provided by the ISP.

Job training and employment. Obtaining and maintaining employment is, like educational achievement, central to the development of self-esteem and the creation of firm bonds to the conventional order. However, at least three factors present major obstacles to the employment prospects of high-risk delinquent youth: their social skills, their technical skills, and the availability of meaningful opportunities. All three areas need to be addressed in ISP.

Programming designed to address social skill deficits would include individualized counseling, and educational and experiential group formats designed to assist youth in job searches, interviews, problem-solving strategies, employer-employee interactions, and communication skills, among others.

Technical skills development needs to be addressed in terms of fundamental academic skills, such as reading, math, and writing, and marketable vocational skills. Skill development in these areas will rely on educational and experiential approaches.

For youth with sufficient basic skills, enrollment in high school vocational programs or community technical schools is an option. For other youth, a focus on continued development of basic academic skills and involvement in work experience programs is essential.

A central focus of phase 2 is the development of employment skills and basic education. A number of programs provide examples of how high-risk youth can be involved in work experience efforts. For example, the Associated Marine Institutes (AMI), based in Tampa, Florida, teaches marine biology, boat repair, and diving. Youth work to repair AMI boats, perform harbor clean-ups, and support environmental projects. Project Green, operated by the New Jersey Juvenile Division, teaches its clients landscape architecture and puts them to work landscaping State and county buildings. In another New Jersey day treatment program, court-adjudicated youngsters run a fast food restaurant, "Jersey Mikes." The youth are involved in the management of the restaurant, and those who successfully complete the program receive a portion of the restaurant's profits. The program attempts to demonstrate that positive results can be achieved from businesses other than drug dealing. Similarly, Maryland's DEAL project prepares and places youth for career ladder jobs in Baltimore City.

The third barrier to employment is the availability of challenging and rewarding job opportunities. While solutions to this problem are beyond the capabilities of ISP, programs can devise strategies for increasing the likelihood of successful job placement. These include tying vocational curriculums and experiences to the needs of the labor market (e.g., AMI's emphasis on marine-related skills in Florida); developing agreements with individual employers to hire youth with relevant interests and aptitudes; and developing supported work programs. An example of the latter strategy is provided by the Youth Advocate Programs (YAP) which place youth into part-time positions that provide vocational

Youth who successfully complete a management program receive a portion of the profits.

Community service and restitution render youth accountable for their behavior.

development opportunities. Wages are paid by YAP, but employers are expected to hire the youth upon successful completion of the training period, usually 2 to 3 months.

Community service/restitution. Several purposes can be served by requiring program youth to participate in community service. First, this method holds youth accountable for their offending behavior and requires them to make concrete amends either directly to the victim via restitution or symbolically to society via community service. Second, community service projects can provide additional structure to a youth's day. Third, well-run programs can provide an environment in which skills transferrable to the work place (e.g., promptness, cooperation, diligence) can be acquired. Finally, ISP community service projects can increase the program's visibility and level of acceptance in the community.

Community service programming should begin in phase 2, the day treatment phase. In many ISP's, this is a daily requirement that provides additional structure to the youth's day. For example, in the Kentfields day treatment program in Grand Rapids, Michigan, the youth, as a group, attend an alternative school in the morning, have lunch at the detention center, and work at a community worksite in the afternoon. Other programs have a weekly requirement, such as the Lucas County, Ohio, ISP, which requires participants to spend 8 hours each Saturday at worksites. For those with large restitution orders, community service work may continue into later program phases.

Substance abuse. The link between substance abuse and chronic delinquent behavior has been well documented. A high-risk population's extensive substance abuse is a reflection of weakened bonds to society and an impediment to efforts to strengthen those bonds. Consequently, this area of service will require considerable attention. Several ISP control elements can be viewed as efforts to deter or restrict opportunity for involvement in drug and alcohol use. In particular, frequent and random urinalysis should be considered a primary control strategy for ISP youth with a history of substance abuse. Obviously, treatment approaches need to complement program controls. Because of the potential influence of substance-abusing behavior on other program interventions, treatment should begin as soon as possible after program entry. For particularly severe cases, completion of a residential substance abuse treatment program should be a prerequisite to acceptance in the ISP.

Recreational/cultural/leisure. Involvement in recreational and cultural activities is usually considered a peripheral activity in correctional programming for delinquents. In the ISP model, this involvement is viewed as a core program element, not so much for the benefits of these activities, such as time management and education, but because youth are exposed to role models and can develop relationships with program staff, nondelinquent peers, and other prosocial forces in the community. While these relationships may develop as a result of other program activities, they are facilitated by leisure activities because the activities themselves are engaging. When a youth is involved in group activities, attachments are more likely to develop than in, for example, a remedial math class. The relationships that may emerge from such activities open an additional avenue to addressing the youth's values and behaviors.

An example is provided by the Chicago Housing Authority's midnight basketball league where the commissioner has become a role model for 18- to 25-year-old project residents. Playing with the high-profile league is not only a source of pride for participants, but also an ongoing course in responsibility and social skills development. One criterion for enrollment is that the person is taking care of a family. Another is that the young men participate in postgame programs designed to help them explore personal responsibility, search for jobs, get along with coworkers, and deal with bosses.

Supportive services

In addition to the core service areas, ISP programming will also need to access specialized services for dealing with the needs of some program participants. These needs are described below.

Residential living. Some family situations will be so chaotic, uncooperative, or so counterproductive that, even with ISP intervention, placement in a group home, foster care, or independent living will be necessary.

Medical/health. For some youth, physical impairments, chronic illness, nutrition problems, or other health issues may be contributing factors to delinquency. These will require specialized services. Other common health issues and concerns, such as AIDS and contraception, should be addressed with all participants.

Mental health. Although many offenders present some mental health needs, a small percentage are seriously emotionally disturbed. Accurate diagnosis, specialized psychiatric/psychological outpatient care, and special ISP staff approaches with this subpopulation will be crucial to successfully integrating youth into the community. The most severely disturbed youth (for example, psychotic) will be excluded from program eligibility. The case management and funding responsibilities of the mental health system should be explicitly outlined.

Special education. Given the high incidence of special education needs among high-risk youth, ISP's will ensure comprehensive educational testing and appropriate educational support services for this subpopulation. In particular, consideration should be given to contracting for the services of a special education teacher to serve youth during phase 2 and to provide ongoing support for those youth reenrolling in public schools.

Special needs offenders. Several additional subgroups of juvenile offenders have recently received increased attention. Predominant among these are developmentally disabled youth and juvenile sex offenders. Because of their prevalence in high-risk populations, intensive supervision programs must have the capability of (1) accurately identifying these subgroups in the assessment process and (2) ensuring that problem-specific services are provided. Without specialized diagnostic and treatment services for these groups (as well as other

The midnight basketball league is an ongoing course in responsibility.

subgroups identified above), core ISP services are likely to have minimal impact. Juvenile sex offenders, for example, are overly compliant with program rules and regulations. This can lead to the belief among staff that such youth are adjusting well to supervision when, in fact, their offenses are continuing.

Summary

This section outlined the key components of the ISP model. Youth move progressively through five phases ranging from a brief secure residential phase to day treatment, outreach and tracking, regular supervision, and program termination.

The critical role of continuous case management must be stressed. Each youth is closely monitored by a case manager who implements a well-defined, individualized regimen, including supervision and services. The case plan results in a behavioral contract between the youth and the case manager. The case plan flows from the initial risk and needs assessment process and is regularly updated by the case manager.

The ISP must pay equal attention to public recognition and rewards for desired conduct as well as timely and appropriate sanctions for rule violations. The sanctioning process must be legitimate and in proportion to the severity of rule violations.

The ISP model emphasizes educational and vocational services. A key objective is to introduce the client to a successful, law-abiding lifestyle. Services will be provided by project staff and will be brokered through other community agencies. Multiagency service networks are very important to program success, and the case manager is responsible for ensuring that high-quality services are provided as specified in the case plan.

Context and implementation

External and internal factors influence how successfully the model can be implemented. The external environment includes the structure of the juvenile justice system in which the program operates, as well as the attributes of the community the program serves. Understanding the importance of these contextual factors can increase the likelihood that policymakers and administrators can plan properly for program implementation. Assessing and dealing with the external environment, the necessary program linkages, and the internal context within which the ISP operates are critical elements to program success.

External environment

The program model is based on the premise that serious youthful offenders can be safely and effectively served in the community after their behavior has been stabilized. This premise must be accepted by policymakers in the local juvenile justice system, both within and outside of the administering agency, for the program to succeed as designed. An ISP will be most effective when it has a broad base of ongoing community support and is used with other community resources.

Administrative support

The first step for program development is to determine the support within the agency for this program model. Do the top administrators within the agency understand and support the program premise? Do they support the program design? Do they support pursuing program development? Are they willing to secure resources for the program? (This will be discussed in more detail later. Although it is anticipated that ISP will be less expensive than training school commitment, startup funding will be needed.)

Second, the need for the program must be determined. What is the impetus for program development? Is this consistent with the program premise? In many communities, rising placement costs and/or crowded facilities are often the impetus, while some States have legislation calling for reduced commitments. These forces would be consistent with the program premise. However, an administration calling for a "get tough" approach for juvenile offenders may want to develop an enhanced probation ISP. They might provide more intensive supervision and/or services to a subset of the probation population, but may not support the diversionary premise of this model.

Besides supporting the program premise, a jurisdiction must be able to divert a sufficient number of long-term, institution-bound juveniles into the program. The comprehensive nature of the program design requires the availability of off-hours surveillance coverage as well as a broad range of services. Without a sufficient number of juveniles meeting the target population criteria, the program could not be properly staffed or cost effective. Therefore, implementing the model as designed would be impractical. The baseline planning study described in the section on Client identification can help make this determination.

Researchers estimate that a jurisdiction would need to enroll a minimum of 60 to 70 juveniles annually in ISP, with an average daily enrollment of 15 in phase 2, in order for full-model implementation. Previous studies (Baird and Neuenfeldt, 1989; Bakal and Krisberg, 1987; DeMunro and Krisberg, 1987) have indicated that when objective classification systems are used to determine which youth need secure care and community-based programs that offer different degrees of structure and types of services, significant proportions of the institutional population have been found appropriate for diversion. As previously noted, 73 percent of the Wisconsin juvenile correctional institution population was identified as suitable for community programming, either directly or following a short-term residential placement. If one estimates that only 30 percent of youth in long-term institutional placements are suitable for ISP, then a jurisdiction with approximately 200 long-term placements annually could have a sufficient number of juvenile offenders for diversion to the ISP.

These figures are estimates only. The percentage of a jurisdiction's out-of-home placement population appropriate for this program would depend on the jurisdiction's current commitment philosophy, policies, and programs. In some

Program development should determine whether a need for the program exists.

jurisdictions, alternative community-based programs already exist, and institutional placement is reserved for those few offenders who pose a serious threat to the community. In other jurisdictions with little programming to offer, the percentages of youth appropriate for the ISP would be greater.

External support

If internal support for the model is present and the need for the program exists, attention must then be devoted to the issue of external support. Support for the ISP must be secured from other juvenile justice policymakers. This support will involve meetings with juvenile court judges, the mayor or county executive, police, prosecutors, public defenders, schools, and community service providers. It may also involve meetings with State juvenile corrections officials and legislators. At the meetings, the program rationale must be explained, along with the strategy for program development. The program design must also be fully described.

Negative reactions to the model should be anticipated because prosecutors may be concerned about leniency, and judges and others may lack faith in the concept. Concerns about public safety in keeping serious juvenile offenders in the community will also be an issue. Funding sources will be concerned about startup costs. The research referenced in this manual can be cited to demonstrate that other jurisdictions have found that effective community-based supervision is achievable, when given the proper structure and resources.

Several key issues will need to be addressed to develop external support. These issues include but are not limited to the structure of the juvenile justice system, fiscal resources, local service agency support, and community attitudes.

Structure of the juvenile justice system. The statutory structure of the juvenile court and the juvenile service delivery system will have an impact on program design and implementation. In some jurisdictions, the juvenile court administers local juvenile justice programs; in others, a county Department of Social Services or Human Services administers the programs. In still other jurisdictions, the State juvenile corrections agency operates local juvenile services programs. In some places, probation or parole staff provide all or nearly all direct services and supervision. Elsewhere, a network of private agencies provides the bulk of services, with probation or parole staff serving as case monitors and managers. Questions of who will make program decisions and who will provide services must be considered during program planning.

In some jurisdictions, judges will directly control who gets into ISP. Even if that is not the case, judicial understanding and support of the program goals and the target population are essential. If judges lack faith in the program, it will be difficult to get the support needed for the program from others within and outside of the juvenile justice system. Several of the ISP's visited to gather information for this guide received considerable judicial support, both in the initial stages of development and on an ongoing basis. Frequently, the judge was a strong ally or the one to secure initial funding. No matter what the structure, the support of juvenile court judges is important to program success. Support from law enforcement, prosecuting attorneys, and public defenders should also be solicited and maintained.

The juvenile justice structure will also impact on the level of State and local cooperation needed under the model. State laws will govern which entity (State or judicial) has the authority to release committed juveniles to ISP. Laws will also dictate which entity has the legal responsibility for the youth while in the program. Program decisions will be controlled locally in jurisdictions where screening and selection processes occur after commitment but before the transfer of authority to the State. In this case, the involvement of State officials is desirable for coordination, program support, and perhaps funding, but is not critical to program implementation.

In jurisdictions where a State corrections agency will administer the program, State and local cooperation is essential. The local jurisdiction will be expected to accept back into the community those youth who had just been deemed inappropriate for community placement. The State agency has the legal responsibility for program clients. Working agreements between local service agencies, such as schools, and the State corrections agency need to be clearly articulated during program development to assure both coordination and accountability. State administrative rules may also have to be modified. The time required for planning and program development under this approach may be longer and should be planned for in the implementation timetable.

Even though startup of ISP in jurisdictions with a State corrections agency structure would entail more planning and coordination efforts, distinct advantages exist. This structure assures the integrity of the target population and would best suit a rigorous evaluation design.[3]

Fiscal resources. The cost of ISP will probably be less than long-term institutional placement; however, significant program startup and maintenance costs may be incurred. Program planners should consider securing funds from the following sources: transfer of funds from the placement budget; reallocation of existing probation resources; the local budgeting process; the State budget process; Federal, State, and local grants; foundation funding; and agreements within and outside the agency to use existing resources for ISP participants.

Who pays for residential placements? In jurisdictions where the State pays for residential costs and local governments pay for local supervision services, there is little financial benefit for communities to establish a comprehensive local services structure. This has led to inappropriate institutional placements of low-risk, nonserious offenders. Some States that had such a funding mechanism have realized the negative public policy aspects and the cost-control disincentives this created and have modified their funding formulas. Juvenile justice costs in most States are funded jointly by State and local sources because cost savings are desirable to both.

---

[3]NCCD recommends that research be conducted to determine the effectiveness of ISP in dealing with serious juvenile offenders. The preferred approach is an experimental research design, with random assignment to the program of those committed juveniles determined appropriate for ISP. A State-administered program would provide the best opportunity for this approach.

S ignificant costs may be incurred to initiate and maintain programs.

Without data to demonstrate that the program is cost effective, long-term funding could be jeopardized.

When local jurisdictions are billed by the State for a portion of the cost of a residential placement, savings to the community by reducing these placements are relatively simple to measure. The cost the State charges a local jurisdiction for an institutional placement can be compared with the average cost for an ISP enrollment. However, the savings to the State may not be as direct. Although the average cost of placements can be readily calculated, the marginal savings from decreased commitments are generally less.[4] Another factor that decreases the calculated cost savings is the number of juveniles who fail on ISP and later end up in a correctional facility. The costs associated with these juveniles will be the costs of both ISP and the correctional facility. For ISP's to be more cost effective than long-term institutional placement at the State level, the program must reduce committed populations to the point where capital expenditures (new construction) and staffing costs in existing institutions are averted or current institutions are closed. To do this, an ISP must achieve a substantial percentage of diversion and must serve as an alternative to long-term institutional placement.

Lucas County (Toledo), Ohio, is an example of how a newly created ISP was funded. The court-run Probation Department established a classification system for juvenile probationers and determined that juveniles with the lowest risk would be on administrative probation and receive no services or supervision. For the next lowest risk juveniles, a program of supervision involving volunteers was established. This left a smaller pool of juveniles requiring probation officer services and allowed the department to transfer a supervisor and three probation officers to the ISP. In addition, the Ohio Department of Youth Service was under a legislative mandate to reduce juvenile commitments and, therefore, provided startup funds for 3 years for the Lucas County program. Finally, Lucas County secured Federal Juvenile Justice Delinquency Prevention Act (JJDPA) startup funds from the Ohio Governor's Office of Criminal Justice Services, which distributes formula JJDPA moneys in Ohio. In this way, Lucas County was able to secure funding for an ISP, even though Ohio has a financial disincentive for local ISP's, because the State pays 100 percent of State training school costs.

Restructuring within the agency to free up existing resources, aggressive pursuit of additional resources through the budget process or grant applications, or some combination will be necessary for program implementation. Once again, political, judicial, and administrative support is important to secure the necessary funding.

Continued support from funding sources must be maintained. This support can be accomplished by demonstrating success in meeting financial goals. Without data to demonstrate that the program is cost effective, long-term funding could be in jeopardy.

---

[4]This is because institutions operate with relatively fixed operating costs. If a system is overloaded or underused on a temporary basis, additional costs or savings are primarily marginal (Funke, n.d.). For example, one cannot assume a direct increase in training school operating costs for each additional juvenile incarcerated above the institution's rated capacity, because additional staff may not be required. In fact, the average cost per juvenile commitment is likely to go down when overcrowding occurs.

Local service agency support. Educational and other community services are key requirements in the program model, and support from these sectors must be generated during program development. Meetings with key agency personnel and policy boards are good ways to inform community agencies about the ISP and generate support. Support of the schools is particularly important, because most ISP youth will need to continue their education. School staff will need to work cooperatively with ISP staff to coordinate educational planning and monitor behavior.

Support from other community programs and groups is also beneficial. Most ISP youth and their families receive services from other community resources. Informing these agencies about the program will assist ISP staff in coordinating services and making appropriate referrals.

Once ISP is implemented, efforts must be made to continue the external support and coordination already established. Without an ongoing effort to inform and communicate, informal support can evaporate.

Community attitudes. Support from the community at large—those outside the juvenile justice system—must be generated as well. The media's response to the proposed program will affect the reactions of the public. Again, concerns about keeping serious juvenile offenders in the community are likely to be raised. A public education effort, aimed at dispelling myths and demonstrating that the program's strong surveillance component will protect the community, should be incorporated into the implementation plan. Presentations describing the program to local victims' organizations may be helpful. Neighborhood associations are also potential allies, and soliciting their support can be helpful. While it may be impossible to generate wholesale support for the program, an effective public education campaign is the best approach to generate program support and minimize misconceptions.

Timing of the public education effort should be considered carefully. Some jurisdictions may want to generate support before implementation, while others may want to keep a low profile until the program has stabilized and positive results can be demonstrated.

The court-run Kentfields program in Grand Rapids, Michigan, is a good example of a program that works hard at communication. Kentfields uses police/court and school/court committees to discuss issues of mutual interest and solve problems. A citizen's advisory council meets once a month to advise the court on matters affecting the community. Staff make speaking engagements to inform the community about the program. The annual report estimates the financial benefit to the community generated by the community service component. Finally, Kentfields solicits donations of gift certificates, movies passes, lunch coupons, and similar items from local merchants, which are used as reinforcers for positive program behavior. These types of donations also let the community know about Kentfields' successes. Program administrators in other jurisdictions will need to identify similar strategies to secure support from these sectors.

The possibility of ISP participants committing a serious crime must be anticipated. Although it is possible to predict the risk of reoffense in the aggregate

Effective public education is the best way to generate program support.

The primary service organization with which linkages must be made is the local school system.

through the use of validated risk assessment instruments, no one can correctly predict the behavior of individuals. The program's risk control strategies are designed to mitigate the likelihood of a serious crime happening. However, strategies should be developed to respond to the media and community if serious offenses occur. Often questions center on the appropriateness of the juvenile's selection into the program, the adequacy of supervision and casework methods, and issues of compliance. If the offender was selected according to policy and was supervised appropriately, an adequate response to public concerns is possible. However, if program policies were not followed, the credibility of the program could be questioned and the future of the program jeopardized (Clear, Holien, and Shapiro, 1989).

Program linkages

The previous section described the external program support that needs to be solicited during program development and maintained afterprogram implementation. This section describes program services requiring operational linkages. Program linkages are both formal and informal relationships with other agencies needed to secure services for clients. These relationships can be with other juvenile justice programs, community programs, and schools. Although programs can survive neutral relationships with some of these entities, negative relationships can be severely detrimental. The comprehensive nature of the services called for by the program requires the coordinated efforts of multiple agencies.

At the individual case level, interagency cooperation is needed for effective program implementation. Thus, formal cooperative interagency agreements that spell out the relationships between agencies are important tools in accomplishing program goals. Formal cooperative agency agreements should establish the parameters of service availability. By definition, the target population for ISP faces many problems, and the assessment and case planning processes will identify service needs that are beyond the scope of ISP. Mechanisms must be in place to ensure referral to and receipt of services identified in the case plan. In too many programs, the only way individual case workers can obtain services for youth is by developing informal relationships with other service providers. Although this informal network can be useful, it cannot substitute for administrative agreements.

Agreements that ensure service slots will be available to ISP clients are important. Too often, services that are supposed to be available are not because of long waiting lists for services, eligibility restrictions, or agencies' unwillingness to accept a difficult population as clientele. Lack of adequate resources will always be a problem. One way to mitigate these difficulties is to obtain commitments from service agencies to set aside a certain number of slots for ISP participants. Because this approach can create problems of its own, administrative support and formal working agreements are needed to make this approach work effectively. Because of the complexity of a multiagency service delivery system, case planning and case management responsibilities that are clearly defined is also crucial.

The primary service organization with which linkages must be made is the local school system. The model calls for a day treatment component, with onsite educational capability. It may be possible for the school district to assign teachers to the program, as in the Kentfields program in Grand Rapids, Michigan, and the Firestone Community Day Center School program in Los Angeles. If ISP hires its own teachers, as do the Associated Marine Institutes in Tampa, Florida, and the State Ward Diversion program in Detroit, Michigan, accreditation of the onsite educational program may need to be obtained. Whether or not the day treatment teachers are employed by the local school district, transition back to the regular school system after day treatment is completed will be necessary for many participants. ISP staff must work with the schools to ensure that the educational goals established in the case plan for each youth are continued or properly modified in later phases. ISP staff may also need to serve as advocates to ensure that the youth is placed in the appropriate school program, such as special education classes or an alternative school. Staff will also need cooperation from the schools for the surveillance aspects of later phases. For example, the Ohio Daily School Report (figure 14) requires ISP participants to obtain written daily observations from each teacher.

School personnel generally support the structure and consistency that ISP's bring to their students' lives, and teachers appreciate the support ISP staff provide when problems in school are encountered. Nevertheless, there will be individual teachers who are not willing to work with ISP staff. In these cases, the formal cooperative agency agreements and administrative support can be used to encourage teacher cooperation.

Other community resources not directly available through ISP such as mental health services, medical resources, drug and alcohol treatment, parental support groups, and legal services will be needed by individual youth and their families. During the program development phase, agencies that provide these services must be identified, and eligibility requirements and mechanisms for obtaining services must be documented.

Community linkages are important as well. For example, YAP, headquartered in Harrisburg, Pennsylvania, considers it a major function to help youth and families develop positive relationships and support systems with their communities and extended family systems. These positive support systems are then in place to assist the youth after YAP participation ends. Support systems can include local YMCA's, Boys Clubs, scouting, church groups, or other community organizations.

The effective use of program linkages is an often overlooked strategy for program development and implementation. ISP is part of a broader network of community resources over which ISP does not have total control. If ISP is to thrive, linkages must be developed and maintained. Therefore, proper attention to this important area will pay dividends in both the program services and administrative areas.

The effective use of program linkages is often overlooked.

A poorly thought-through program cannot be well implemented.

Internal linkages

Internal linkages are the organizational conditions and administrative policies and procedures necessary to implement ISP successfully. They include administrative commitment and staff buying; the location of ISP in the agency structure; and the policies and procedures governing program operations, including fiscal and personnel. Because the ISP model must be tailored to fit local circumstances, many operational issues are left to local resolution. These issues need to be addressed in detail during implementation planning and incorporated in policy and procedure statements.

Conditions

Agency philosophy and administrative commitment. An agency philosophy that supports the program premise is critical to success. This philosophy is especially true when the ISP represents a significant departure from conventional operations. Top administrative commitment enables proper development and integration, oversight, funding, and training. Administrators or staff should not view ISP as the latest fad that will enhance the agency's stature. The program is designed to meet a chronic need of the juvenile justice system and should therefore be considered a permanent component of that system.

Staff buying. The agency mission statement and ISP program premise should be disseminated to all staff. A series of internal staff meetings to explain the program and address staff concerns should be held, similar to those for outside groups. Negative points raised by staff should not be ignored or dismissed, but addressed within the program design, if possible. Where accommodation and adaptation are not feasible, the rationale for the decision should be made explicit.

The attitudes of traditional probation officers toward ISP can affect program success. Particularly in probation-run programs, resentment from traditional probation officers toward ISP officers can be a management problem. Administrators must work hard to mitigate these frictions.

Staff participation in program development. Staff participation in program planning encourages commitment and ensures that the program is grounded in reality. The preferred approach is to establish a working committee to refine the design and to develop an implementation plan, including a budget and timetable. The committee should represent a cross-section of agency staff, including line, supervisory, and administrative personnel. It might also include key people from outside the agency such as judges, police officers, and community service providers. Organizing such a committee should be considered a major organizational development effort, and priority for the project should be given accordingly.

Adequate planning time. The ISP model presents complex and demanding design and implementation issues. Pressures to get the program up and running should be strongly resisted. A poorly thought-through program cannot be well implemented. **A minimum of 6 months should be allowed for the program planning process.**

Operational issues

Agency organization and the juvenile justice structure vary considerably among agencies, and this variety is built into the model design. The ISP model must be tailored to fit into each agency's service delivery system and its internal policies and procedures. The following operational issues are discussed briefly: organizational structure, congruence with current policies and procedures, staff roles and competencies, and fiscal issues. This list is by no means complete, and in developing an operations manual, other issues specific to the agency should be considered.

Organizational structure. Perhaps the biggest operational issue is whether or not the ISP is operated by a private contractor or by the staff of the administering agency. As part of its assessment, NCCD conducted site visits to programs operated by probation departments and private programs under contract with State or county agencies. Three private programs were included in the site visits: KEY, Inc., headquartered in Framingham, Massachusetts; Associated Marine Institutes, Inc., headquartered in Tampa, Florida; and Youth Advocate Programs, Inc., headquartered in Harrisburg, Pennsylvania. In addition, the Wayne County (Detroit), Michigan, ISP included two private providers—Spectrum Human Services, Inc., and the Comprehensive Youth Training and Community Involvement Program, Inc. (CYTCIP).

The strength of all the private programs was their ability to provide a variety of services tailored to the needs of their clients and to respond quickly to the need for new programming. Private providers generally have greater internal staffing and administrative flexibility than government-operated programs. For example, KEY requires a college degree for its line staff, but only allows these staff to be in their positions for 14 months. KEY rotates staff more quickly than most public personnel systems and therefore maintains a consistently high-quality line staff who move on before burning out. The State contracting agency viewed this practice as a significant strength.

Another example of flexibility is the Youth Advocate Programs, which provides intensive services to youth and families through an advocacy model. With an average caseload of four youth, advocates spend a minimum of 7.5 hours and a maximum of 30 hours a week with each youth, generally on nights and weekends. Quickly matching a youth with an advocate based on the youth's interests, needs, and location is crucial to the program design. Because advocates are not full-time employees and 70 percent have another full- or part-time job, YAP has recruited a pool of advocates for rapid assignment of youths. Reassignments can be made quickly if a match does not work.

The ISP model calls for staff coverage 7 days a week, 16 hours a day. Although this can be accommodated in probation-run programs (both the Lucas County, Ohio, and the Hennepin County, Minnesota, programs have probation staff coverage on evenings and weekends), staff coverage tends to be more problematic in civil service systems. Issues raised during the assessment included pay differentials and seniority rights. For example, during the development of ISP in Allegheny County, Pennsylvania, probation staff initially were reluctant to volunteer to work during nontraditional hours, and both union and personnel

The strength of private programs is their ability to provide a variety of services tailored to their clients.

The need for a multiplicity of core services and extensive and flexible staff coverage makes private contracting preferable.

rules prohibited reassignment. Administrative and judicial support for the program was persuasive enough to eventually solicit enough volunteers to begin the program. These problems were not evident in the privately run programs.

The perceptions of regular probation staff that the ISP gets special treatment from the administration and priority for service slots can also be a source of conflict in probation-run programs. Although management can minimize these problems, the friction inherent in the organizational structure cannot be totally eliminated.

The advantage of probation-operated ISP's is that administrative costs can be shared with other juvenile justice services, thereby minimizing direct program costs. However, the sharing of costs makes determination of the true program costs more difficult. More important, public programs have more control than private programs over policy and funding decisions. Often private providers have little input into programmatic and funding changes that significantly affect service delivery. Access to key policymakers, including juvenile judges, may also be more difficult for private providers.

Although both the private and public approaches have advantages and disadvantages, private contracting is preferable for the ISP model because of the need for a multiplicity of core services and extensive and flexible staff coverage. This arrangement is not to say that the ISP model cannot be adapted by public agencies. For example, the court-run Kentfields program in Grand Rapids, Michigan, contains many of the elements described in this model. Kentfields has a day treatment component with alternative schooling, group counseling, community service, and recreational activities. It operates on a "token economy" system, where points earned for positive performance can be redeemed for a paycheck and for restitution payments. Finally, the aftercare phase gradually reduces both the program requirements and the reinforcers, which have effectively controlled the youth's behavior.

Although private contracting is the suggested approach, the overall context of the administering agency and the needs of the juvenile justice system will determine the best operating structure for individual jurisdictions.

Congruence with current policy and procedures. The extent to which ISP policies and procedures conflict with those of the larger organization and the external environment must be considered. If conflicts are identified, efforts must be made to make the ISP policies congruent. For example, the use of short-term detention may raise issues of administrative versus judicial authority in decisionmaking. Other questions that might be raised include: Is it appropriate for ISP staff to have access to detention beds when other probation staff do not? How can program needs be reconciled with those of overcrowded detention facility administrators? Conflicts over policies such as these must be carefully negotiated to ensure continuing external support for the program, without compromising fundamental program principles.

Staff roles. Different staff functions are needed for different program phases. For example, teachers are needed during the day treatment phase and, perhaps, the residential/incarceration phase (phases 1 and 2), with youth transferring to the regular school system in later phases. Case managers are assigned to youth throughout all the phases, while trackers are needed only for the day treatment and outreach and tracking phases (phases 2 and 3). Staff are needed for supervising community service work and for individual, group, and family counseling. The multiplicity of roles and variety of methods used during the separate phases make proper staffing a complex issue.

An example of a possible staffing pattern that meets the caseload standards identified in the Intervention section is presented below. In this example, it is assumed that program enrollment is 50, divided among the phases as follows:

Phase	Enrollment
Phase 1	5
Phase 2	15
Phase 3	15
Phase 4	15

Staffing
1 Teacher
3 Case managers/counselors
2 Trackers (nights and weekends)
1 Teaching assistant/driver/community service work crew supervisor
1 Administrator (half-time direct service)
1 Clerical
9 Staff; 7.5 direct service staff

Client-to-direct service staff ratio	6.67:1
Client-to-case manager ratio	16.67:1
Client-to-tracker ratio	15:1
Client-to-teacher ratio	15–20:1
Client-to-teacher/teacher aide ratio	7.5–10:1

This manual gives some direction for types of staff needed (case managers, counselors, teachers, and surveillance officers) and caseload ratios, but program developers will need to focus in greater detail on this important area. Staff roles need to be defined to make expectations clearly understood. In large part, staff roles and functions translate program design into program execution.

The role of ISP case managers can range from pure case manager and service broker to direct service provider. In practice, it is likely that case managers will develop a style that blends the broker and direct service roles. Job variation in emphasis across sites and even among staff within sites is also likely. These variations result from differences in an agency's traditional practices, the availability of community resources, and the preferences of ISP staff. For example, in areas where community resources are limited, ISP staff may have to rely on inhouse substance abuse treatment or family counseling. In contrast, in relatively resource-rich communities, the service broker role might be more appropriate.

Regardless of variations, the ISP model requires case managers to perform certain core functions. First, one case manager should have primary responsibility throughout a youth's program stay. Second, case managers should have primary responsibility for assessment, case planning, and the coordination of services.

Staff roles and functions translate program design into program execution.

Case managers should create partnerships with parents.

Third, through the application of a reward/sanction system that is tied to daily behavior, case managers should be extensively involved in micromanaging youth. Counseling tied to daily behavior will be more frequent, more proactive, and more sharply focused than that typically found in probation supervision. Finally, case managers should play an active role in relation to people and institutions in the community because of the need to develop prosocial bonds, develop a community support network, and provide opportunities for youth. Creating partnerships on behalf of youth with parents, schools, and employers will constitute a significant part of the case manager's role.

The role of surveillance or tracking staff may also be conceptualized along a continuum, ranging from the big brother or sister to the pure police model. As with case managers, some blending and balancing of these two roles is likely and desirable. On the one hand, surveillance and tracking staff have primary responsibility for monitoring and reporting youth's compliance with program conditions. This is an indispensable role and one which necessarily emphasizes the "cop" function. On the other hand, the frequent interaction between surveillance staff and youth and family members has typically promoted a high level of trust and created opportunities for formal and informal counseling interventions.

Other ISP functions suggest fairly straightforward roles. Day treatment teachers, mentors, family advocates, and community service work supervisors all have unique roles. However, some of these roles may be combined with others in any one staff person's job. Surveillance staff might also be responsible for overseeing community service work. Family advocates or community service supervisors might also serve as counselors or teacher's aides within the day treatment program.

Persons serving in these ISP roles may have different relationships to the program. While case managers will be full-time agency employees, surveillance staff may be contractors, day treatment teachers may be on loan from the public schools, and mentors may be volunteers.

Because of the range of roles played by staff and their differing relationships to the program, considering all ISP-related staff as part of a supervision and intervention team is crucial. The team approach will require the following: (1) extensive formal and informal communication channels, (2) a high level of coordination of tasks (typically by the case manager), and (3) close attention to the delineation of staff roles and responsibilities. Care must be taken to identify the boundaries of full-time ISP staff roles as well as those of staff who will be interacting frequently with ISP youth. For example, the relative authority of case managers and surveillance staff in determining consequences, and that of case managers and program specialists (for example, substance abuse specialists) in making referrals will need to be defined. Other responsibilities also need to be resolved. In particular, what is the authority and the responsibility of auxiliary staff such as mentors and family advocates?

Staff competencies. Once roles have been defined, the issue of competencies must be addressed. How can the program ensure that staff have the commitment and the skills to carry out the program? This question covers a range of issues, including selection, training, and incentives. The rigors of intensively supervising high-risk and hard-core delinquents demand special characteristics. At a minimum, staff must be highly motivated, committed, and energetic.

Case managers typically have had several years of experience; have demonstrated a blend of toughness, street smarts, and care for youth; and have developed effective working relationships with community agencies. Many of these same characteristics are sought in day treatment staff. Good surveillance staff may come from varied backgrounds and may be former students, detention personnel, or police officers. Many programs hire surveillance staff who reside in, or are very comfortable moving about, high-crime neighborhoods. This approach reflects a dual concern for familiarity with street culture and staff safety. In one site, a former "repo man" was hired as a surveillance officer. He was able to work in the toughest neighborhoods because most community residents already knew him and accepted him as an enforcer.

The intervention strategies posited by the ISP model will likely require extensive ongoing training whether staff are hired from within the facility or from the outside. Primary training areas include the following: (1) dealing with unique subpopulations such as drug dealers and sex offenders, (2) performing behavior-specific case planning and contracting, (3) using graduated rewards and sanctions, (4) ensuring officer safety, and (5) helping parents reestablish control over their teenagers. Finally, many staff members will probably not be accustomed to the frequent interactions demanded by ISP and may not know how to use their time productively. They will need to learn ways of maximizing the benefits of increased contacts.

Sustaining high levels of commitment and motivation will be difficult even with the most energetic of staff. Burnout is a pressing issue, and policies to address it must be promulgated. Staff need concrete incentives such as higher pay, liberal rules for compensation time, and flexible work schedules to compensate both for evening and weekend work and the psychological pressures of ISP work. Although ISP work carries with it its own intangible rewards—a sense of mission, of being able to do probation the way it was meant to be done—these tend to fade over time. Typically, civil service systems may not be flexible enough to provide extra pay for ISP officers, to allow them to work evening and weekend hours, or to make adjustments for erratic work schedules. Such disincentives might be balanced partially by the sense of mission, innovation, and esprit de corps engendered by ISP operations. However, it is likely that the issue of concrete incentives will remain whether the program is privately or publicly operated.

Another method for preventing burnout involves periodic rotation of staff into and out of ISP. This method has worked extremely well for KEY. However, it places additional burdens on staff recruitment, training, and supervision. Another way to maintain motivation is through informal support networks. In some locations ISP staff have developed networks with ISP workers in other jurisdictions. Supportive activities may be as minimal as occasional phone conversations and joint attendance at conferences or as extensive as formal cross-training.

The rigors of intensive supervision make burnout a pressing issue.

Program designs that look good on paper often fail during implementation.

Fiscal. Fiscal policies and procedures need to be in place to ensure appropriate use of financial resources, provide program accountability, and establish documentation for program monitoring and evaluation. Fiscal procedures should be documented and communicated to all parties, including program and agency administrators, funding sources, and subcontractors. Failure to do so may hinder operations or cause loss of credibility with people in the external environment. For example, in one program a major conflict arose between ISP and the State funding agency over the use of funds for out-of-home placement for ISP youth. Neither group had anticipated the need for such placements and consequently had no budget categories or method for paying these costs. ISP paid for these unanticipated costs out of its own budget, straining other budgeted services.

Summary

Proper consideration of these and other internal and external linkage issues may mean the difference between success and failure. All too often, program designs that look good on paper fail during implementation because real-world constraints have not been properly accommodated. The external and internal forces affecting a program can hinder operations. However, if properly addressed, they can also be used to a program's advantage.

Goals and evaluation

Each agency implementing ISP must articulate program goals and establish proper client tracking, program monitoring, and process evaluation procedures. If the model is to truly demonstrate the fundamental premise that serious youthful offenders can be safely and effectively served in the community after their behavior has been stabilized, then an additional component—outcome evaluation—must be designed and implemented. This chapter sets forth basic principles of goal setting, management information, process evaluation, and outcome evaluation that must be considered as part of the program planning phase.

Demonstration goals

The essential goal of implementation is to demonstrate that the ISP model can manage large numbers of serious juvenile offenders at no greater risk to the community than long-term institutional placement and at lower cost. Agencies implementing the model also must establish their own long-range program goals and corresponding measurable objectives in the areas of participant outcome and cost effectiveness.

Program goals

Goals are broad statements of purpose, and as such, are general statements of what a program should accomplish. Within the context of the overall ISP goals, agency-specific goals should address local needs and have the necessary political and community support to achieve them. The compelling problems leading to the creation of ISP should be reflected in the program goals. Finally, the program goals should relate to the agency mission. Because program goals are statements of intent, most programs have no more than three goals.

Goals should specify the condition to be altered—that is, provide a lower cost alternative to long-term institutional placement with no greater risk to the community and the target population (serious juvenile offenders) of the program. Well thought-out goals should provide a clear understanding of the scope of the program, form the foundation for the development of objectives, and suggest a set of possible program strategies. For example, the public protection part of the model goal implies program strategies involving some form of supervision and control.

Program objectives

After program goals have been established, measurable objectives must be set for each goal. This step is important, because decisions on how to measure achievement will be used in the design of the management information and evaluation systems. Similar to individual case planning, the focus of program objectives should be on outcomes—on what is to be accomplished. Process objectives, which specify activities, are more appropriately covered in the section on methods. For example, the objective, "All juveniles committed to the State training school will be assessed for ISP enrollment," is a process step that does not specify what outcome is to be achieved. On the other hand, the objective, "Sixty percent of ISP clients terminating in 1990 will successfully complete the program, as measured by no new adjudications," is specific as to anticipated result.

To be measurable, an objective must specify what change is to be achieved, who will achieve it, within what timeframe, and what proportion of the target population is expected to show the change or what amount of change is expected. For example, a cost-effectiveness objective may be, "By the end of the second year of implementation, the average cost per ISP participant will be 25-percent less than the average cost of a training school placement." (It should be noted that the average cost comparison may not truly measure the cost savings of a program. This issue would be measured in an outcome evaluation effort.)

Objectives should be realistic, should be based on reasonable timelines, and should be within the control of those responsible. Once established, all staff in the agency and in participating service provider agencies should receive copies of the goals and objectives, along with the strategy for measuring achievement. A clear understanding of what the program is to accomplish is essential for all staff to work consistently toward a common goal.

After program goals have been established, measurable objectives must be set.

Management information system

Overview

To demonstrate that the ISP model can manage serious juvenile offenders at no greater risk and at lower cost to the community than long-term institutional placement, information must be available to measure the objectives related to this overall goal. The types of information needed include (1) juvenile characteristics and offense histories (what constitutes a serious juvenile offender?); (2) program interventions (what strategies were used, and what were the results?); (3) outcomes (what offenses and rules violations occurred during program enrollment and during followup, and how does this compare with a similar group of youth in long-term institutional placement?); and (4) fiscal data (what are the actual costs of ISP, and what would have been spent for long-term institutional placement?). Besides client-specific information, data are needed for managers to track such things as enrollments, terminations, and lengths of stay. Without a properly designed and properly operating management information system (MIS), demonstration of program and cost effectiveness is unlikely to be achieved. This section will describe the requirements for an MIS and discuss system design and development issues.

Two functional areas must be included in the MIS: (1) program data, which are aggregate management data; and (2) client tracking data, which track individual clients through the program.

Although an MIS can have varying levels of automated capability and take on a variety of configurations, its primary purpose is to provide management with the information needed to guide decisionmaking. Although MIS components will facilitate the day-to-day staff tasks, the primary goal must be to support broad management and reporting needs. The agency management process is illustrated in figure 16.

Management information is needed throughout the continuum—for policy formation, planning and operational decisions, monitoring and process evaluation, and outcome evaluation. As shown in figure 16, agency goals are translated into policy statements, which in turn lead to planning and operational decisions. Operations are then monitored and evaluated. The feedback loop implies that reports are generated to provide the necessary information gathered in the monitoring and evaluation processes. Another word for feedback is output—what information is contained in the reports and in what format.

Client tracking data are organized into discreet sections: information about the juvenile and his or her family, offense history, risk and needs assessment results, progress in program, and termination and followup information. These data are generally more useful to line staff and supervisors, although some client tracking data can be aggregated for management use.

MIS design

In designing an MIS, two fundamental issues must be addressed: (1) What data are needed? and (2) How and when should data be collected and processed?

Figure 16: Agency Management Process

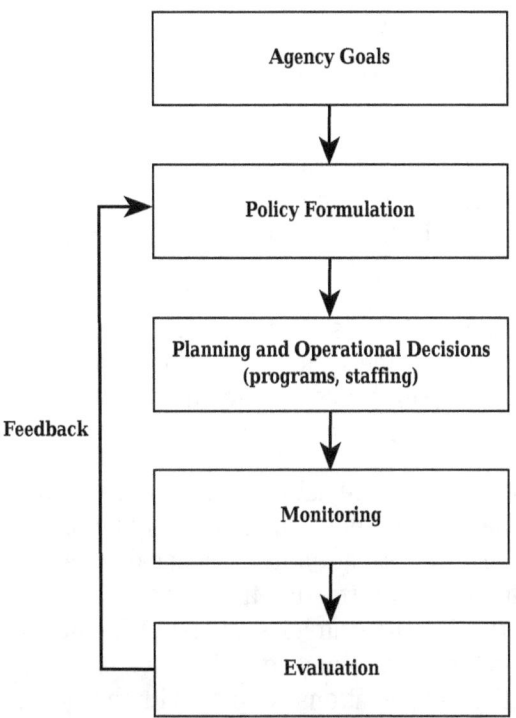

The first step in MIS design is defining data needs.

The first step in MIS design is defining data needs for reports, documents, listings, statistics, and rapid inquiry. These data represent what staff need to know and what managers want to know about operations. The use of an MIS is not measured by how much data are put into the system, but by how useful the outputs are. Therefore, MIS design should be approached from the standpoint of identifying what is needed to operate and evaluate the program. The selection of data elements required for client tracking, planning, budgeting, monitoring, and evaluating is not easy. Some agencies collect too much information, and consequently the accuracy and timeliness of the data are inadequate. Other agencies collect too little information and are unable to adequately plan or evaluate programs or policies without collecting additional data through staff surveys or other expensive, time-consuming means.

In identifying data needs, working from general to specific is helpful, using the following approach:

- Describe the output reports needed in general terms.
- Identify who needs which reports how often.
- Identify the data elements needed for each report.
- Identify the desired format.
- Identify inquiry needs and unique data elements.

Unless it can be accurately defined, a data element should be excluded.

The following questions should be kept in mind throughout these procedures:

- To what activity or function is it related?

- How will the data element be used, and who will benefit from its inclusion?

- How will it be captured? On what form? How will the form be routed through the data entry person?

The presumption should be to exclude a data element unless function, benefit, and capture can be accurately defined. The possibility that it might be useful in the future is usually inadequate justification. Every data element selected should have a practical purpose.

An MIS work group, consisting of line staff, managers, and technical MIS personnel should be formed to design the system. MIS staff can learn from program staff what information is critical and how to create a comprehensive systems design that will aid in the programming effort.

In designing an information system, the natural temptation is to get everything at once, to solve all information problems simultaneously by making a quantum leap from no information to all information. Experience dictates that this is not a wise approach. Collecting more information than is needed drains staff resources, is more likely to result in inaccuracies and reporting delays, and may result in less information being used. Many agencies have monthly printouts, which are ignored. Unrealistic expectations coupled with the system's failure to produce timely, accurate, and useful data lead to cynicism and staff resistance to data collection procedures.

When determining data requirements, an agency must also consider various processing options, which are discussed below. Automated data needs drive software needs, which in turn drive hardware needs. Because every MIS hardware configuration (mainframes, minis, and micros) contains strengths and weaknesses, hardware constraints (if any) should be known at the start of the design process.

Some phases of a well-designed system may operate on a manual basis while other phases should be automated. Choosing which data need to be computerized and which do not is the key to developing an efficient information system. Although generalities seldom apply in total to an agency, experience in systems development in many organizations has led to the following guidelines for selecting appropriate processing options for each module of an information system.

Manual systems are in some instances the most efficient means to process information that need not be aggregated. Reports that can be efficiently produced manually include lists of case actions due in a specific period of time, case plans, and the frequency and types of contacts. Although reminder lists are important to line staff and supervisors, many agencies have well-designed manual systems that produce these listings.

A manual system with batch processing of summary data can also be an efficient option. Some tracking procedures can be done effectively manually and still provide valuable aggregate data for management. An agency must weigh the cost of automating an entire process against the cost of keying in manually tabulated summaries on a weekly, monthly, or less frequent basis. Though this option is seemingly unsophisticated, its simplicity and minimal cost make it the best approach in many situations. The primary drawback is the time lag that occurs between staff actions, summaries, and data entry. Therefore, this option should only be used for routine reports for which a short delay in obtaining the data is of little consequence to management.

Automation should be used for data that will be aggregated for management use. In addition, automated client tracking systems can be of great use to line staff and supervisors. The most successful systems are based on simple designs. Recent advances in technology (that is, the microprocessor) have created new opportunities for automated data management. Microcomputers now have the capacity to meet the needs of nearly all juvenile corrections agencies, which frees them from centralized data processing operations and allows them to have control over the collection, processing, and reporting of data. Microcomputer-based processing operations are quickly replacing centralized operations in other fields and should be considered by all juvenile corrections organizations.

In summary, a good data system is essential to good management. An effective, comprehensive MIS possesses the following attributes:

- Uses a combination of manual, batch processing, and online applications to meet agency needs (although microcomputers and distributive processing are resulting in increased automation).

- Captures data from forms used for other purposes rather than adding a new layer of paperwork.

- Is dynamic and flexible. Information items and report formats can be added, changed, or deleted without major programming.

- Provides aggregate information routinely to management. (Management use of this information should, in turn, be conveyed to line staff.)

- Provides timely and useful information to all levels of the organization and is integrally tied to other management functions.

- Protects the integrity of data by incorporating routine editing procedures (manual and/or automated).

Data elements

Many data elements serve both client tracking and program management. For example, phase completion dates indicate to line staff which clients are in a particular phase of the program and provide management with the numbers of clients in each phase at a given time along with their length-of-stay averages. Although the data elements listed below are typical, individual agencies need to follow the design steps listed above to determine their specific needs.

Microcomputer-based processing operations should be considered.

C ollecting more information than is needed drains staff resources.

1. Intake and Assessment Information

Client Demographics

- Name.
- Birth date.
- Sex.
- Race.
- Address.
- Phone number.
- Social security number.
- School name (if any).
- School address.
- Contact person at school.
- School phone number.
- Employer's name (if any).
- Address of employer.
- Phone number of employer.

Parents or Guardian and Siblings

- Names of parents or guardian.
- Relationship to client.
- Address.
- Phone number.
- Employer.
- Work phone.
- Marital status.
- Sibling names.
- Sibling ages.

Offense History

- Disposition date.
- Committing offense and date.
- Adjudicated offense(s).
- Offense(s) charged at arrest (if different from adjudication).
- Detention at arrest?
- Current placement status.
- Number of prior delinquency referrals.
- Prior adjudicated offenses and dates.

Risk Assessment *(from Risk Assessment Scale in figure 4)*

- Date of assessment.
- Age at first adjudication.
- Number of prior arrests.
- Current offense.
- Number of prior out-of-home placements.
- History of drug usage.
- Current school status.
- Probation status.
- Number of runaways from prior placements.
- Number of grades behind in school.
- Level of parental/caretaker control.
- Peer relationships.

Needs Assessment *(from Needs Scale in figure 5)*

- Date of assessment.
- Basic living situation.
- Primary family relationships.
- Alternative family relationships.
- Emotional stability.
- Peer relationships.
- Substance abuse.
- Victimization.
- Intellectual ability.
- School adjustment.
- Employment.
- Vocational or technical skills.
- Transportation.
- Health, hygiene, and personal appearance.
- Runaway history.
- Victim of abuse/neglect.
- School status.
- Truancy history.
- Prior placements.

2. Client Progress in Program

- Phase completion dates.
- Services received (type and date).
- Academic gain.
- Rules violation (type and date).
- Program sanctions (type and date).
- Living arrangements.
- Arrests (type and date).
- Risk and needs reassessments.
- Staff assigned.

3. Termination

- Date of termination.
- Reason for termination.
- Legal status.

- Living arrangement.
- School status.
- Employment status.
- Assessment of progress.

4. Followup data (6 or 12 months following termination)

- Date of followup.
- Number of arrests.
- Number of adjudications or convictions.
- Legal status.
- Living arrangement.
- School status.
- Employment status.

An MIS containing the program management and case tracking functions described above is an essential part of the ISP model. In recent years, technology has been developed that enables even small agencies to procure the systems needed to manage cases and programs. This important component should not be overlooked.

Evaluation

ISP demonstration programs should plan for a program evaluation that consists of two phases. Phase 1 will assess the program's planning and implementation processes (process evaluation) and refine the outcome evaluation design. Phase 2 will continue the process evaluation and will also incorporate an outcome evaluation using experimental and control groups.

Process evaluation

The goals of the process evaluation are to describe how the program operates and the forces impeding, facilitating, or modifying the model's implementation as designed. The process evaluation will comprehensively describe ISP and analyze how it was conceptualized, planned, and implemented. If applicable, the evaluation will then systematically describe how each program element was changed. The description of program design and changes should be followed by a description of the political and social forces that forced such changes to be made. This prescription has no assumption that such political and social forces are necessarily improper or address other than program needs, although that could be the case.

Preferably, an organization without institutional links to the program should conduct the evaluation. If the evaluation is to be conducted by a parent or affiliate of the program, the proposed design should describe how objectivity will be maintained and how situations of conflicts in loyalty to the needs of the institution and the needs of the evaluation will be avoided.

> Technology enables even small agencies to procure the systems needed to manage cases and programs.

The process evaluation will comprehensively describe the intensive supervision program.

The program elements to be analyzed during the process evaluation are described below:

■ Context—the set of conditions and assumptions that operationally and conceptually define the distinctive features of the program. In discussing the former, the evaluation is very likely to address some of the institutional constraints and pressures that shape and modify the program. Examples of questions to be examined in this area include:

  ☐ What philosophies guided planned interventions?

  ☐ What conditions in the local juvenile justice system did the program address?

  ☐ Who were the key participants in proposing and approving the program's formation?

■ Client identification—the combination of techniques, procedures, and criteria employed to define, select, and admit clients to various levels of service and supervision provided by the program. Examples of questions to be examined in this area include:

  ☐ What are the formal procedures for selecting clients and how does actual practice diverge from these?

  ☐ Under what conditions do program personnel diverge from selection procedures?

  ☐ To what extent do participants reflect the target population?

■ Program interventions—the full range of services and activities provided by the program to meet the needs of clients. Among questions to be examined in this area are:

  ☐ To what extent do clients participate in the different program interventions?

  ☐ What program interventions were planned but not executed and for what reasons?

  ☐ What are clients' and program staff is attitudes toward each intervention?

■ Goals and evaluation—an assessment of whether program operations are consistent with the goals and the criteria used to determine how effective the program is in meeting its objectives. (Evaluation here refers to a program management function, not to the formal process of assessing institutional viability and effectiveness.) Examples of questions to be examined in this area include:

  ☐ What criteria do program administrators use to assess the effectiveness of program interventions? How do these differ between staff, managers, and clients?

  ☐ How do staff, program administrators, and clients perceive program goals? In what ways do definitions diverge?

■ Program linkages—the formal and informal conditions and relationships that may hinder or support program operations. An assessment of these conditions is likely to reveal some of the institutional constraints and influences that shaped the program's design and implementation. The following questions are to be examined in this area:

- What are the attitudes toward the program among staff and administrators in other units of the parent organization? For example, do probation officers in other units view the program positively or negatively?

- How is the program viewed among other organizations in the juvenile justice system? What are the attitudes of prosecutors, public defenders, judges, and police toward the program?

- Has the program built cooperative relationships with other agencies that provide or potentially provide services to clients?

In analyzing the program's operations and the forces impinging upon implementation, the evaluation should focus on the degree of internal consistency among program elements and on the program developmental stages (Krisberg, 1980):

- Consistency of program elements—an assessment of the extent to which program elements are logically and empirically related. Many of the sample questions suggested above imply a focus on program consistency. More to the point, research questions should be asked that probe the logic of all the program elements. For example, client selection criteria and program interventions should reflect the program's philosophy, referral mechanisms should reflect the clients' selection criteria, and so forth.

- Program stages—the four stages of development: planning, implementation, operations, and if applicable, institutionalization. The evaluation should examine how context, interventions, and other program elements change across stages and explain how these changes in external conditions impinge upon the program.

Outcome evaluation

The ISP outcome evaluation will examine three areas: the extent to which the ISP group reduced law-violating behavior, the extent to which it increased clients' positive adjustment, and costs. Positive adjustment refers to participation in educational, occupational, family, and community activities that provide youth with positive reasons to abstain from criminal behavior. The ISP theoretical model and other delinquency research explain how participation in these activities is expected to reduce criminal behavior. To determine whether the program is effective in reducing law-violating behavior and increasing the youth's positive adjustment, an experimental study is required. In the experimental study, outcome measures will be gathered for program clients in comparison with a randomly selected group of youth who were eligible for the program, but who were placed in traditional residential programs.

The evaluation design will propose and justify a set of criminal and rehabilitation outcome measures. Among important justification criteria are the measures' relevance to program goals and their validity (the degree to which they represent actual client behavior and attitudes, which the program is trying to change).

Evaluation should take into account how the program is viewed by juvenile justice professionals.

The need for
juvenile intensive
supervision has never
been greater.

Among law-violating behavior measures to be considered are: self-reported delinquency and drug use, types and seriousness of arrest charges, and juvenile justice dispositions arising from such arrests. The design should specify how the analysis will treat juvenile justice dispositions stemming from youth's performance while in the program (e.g., return to a residential facility because of misbehavior or noncompliance).

Among rehabilitative measures that may be proposed are the degree of participation in educational programs (for example, attendance, completion), improvements in reading and mathematics scores, amount of time spent in employment and income earned, gains in attitudes and motivations related to successful job seeking and retention, satisfaction with family and law-abiding friends, self-esteem, and perceived control over life.

Outcome evaluation by an independent research group is imperative. Program administrators must also support the random assignment methods if the research results are to be valued.

Conclusion

The need for juvenile intensive supervision has never been greater, given the current overloaded and underfunded juvenile justice system. The cost of institutional placement continues to climb, reaching as high as $57,500 a year (Allen-Hagen, 1991).

NCCD is developing training curriculums to support this implementation manual. The operations manual and training materials combined with the previously published site-visit summaries and assessment report will provide a sufficient base of information to encourage the development of this ISP approach throughout the juvenile justice field.

References

Allen-Hagen, Barbara (1991). "Public Juvenile Facilities Children in Custody 1989." *Juvenile Justice Bulletin*, January.

Andrews, Don (1987)." Implications of Classification for Treatment of Juveniles." Paper presented to the American Probation and Parole Association. Salt Lake City, Utah, August.

Baird, Christopher, and Deborah Neuenfeldt (1990). "The Client Management Classification System." NCCD *FOCUS*, August.

Baird, Christopher, and Deborah Neuenfeldt (1989). "Juvenile Corrections in Wisconsin: Is There A Better Way?" NCCD *FOCUS*, September.

Baird, Christopher, and Todd Clear (1986). *In/Out Decisionmaking: A Conceptual Framework*. Washington, D.C.: National Institute of Corrections.

Bakal, Yitzhak, and Barry Krisberg (1987). *Placement Needs for Youth Committed to Oregon Training Schools*. San Francisco: NCCD.

Barton, William H., and Jeffrey Butts (1988). *The Metro-County Intensive Supervision Experiment: Project Brief, Selected Results From a Five-Year Program Evaluation*. Ann Arbor: University of Michigan, Institute for Social Research.

Clear, Todd R. (1988). "Statistical Prediction in Corrections." *Research in Corrections*, March.

Clear, Todd R. (1986). *Juvenile Intensive Probation Supervision: Theory and Rationale*. Paper presented at JIPS Symposium, Minneapolis, Minnesota, October 19–22.

Clear, Todd R. (n.d.). *Objectives-Based Case Planning*. Unpublished.

Clear, Todd R., and Patricia L. Hardyman (1990). "The New Intensive Supervision Movement." *Crime and Delinquency*, January.

Clear, Todd R., Douglas A. Holien, and Carol Shapiro (1989). *Developing Intensive Supervision Programs: A Practitioner's Guide*. Madison, Wisconsin: NCCD.

Coates, Robert, Alden Miller, and Lloyd Ohlin (1978). *Diversity in a Youth Correctional System*. Cambridge: Ballinger.

DeMunro, Paul, and Barry Krisberg (1987). *Adjudicated Youth in Delaware Who Need Secure Care*. San Francisco: NCCD.

Elliott, Delbert, David Huizinga, and Susan Ageton (1985). *Explaining Delinquency and Drug Use*. Beverly Hills, California: Sage Publications.

Empey, Lamer, and Steven Lubeck (1971). *The Silverlake Experiment: Testing Delinquency Theory and Community Intervention*. Aldine.

Erwin, Billie S. (1986). *Final Report of the Georgia Intensive Probation Supervision Project*. Atlanta: Department of Corrections.

Funke, Gail S. "The Economics of Prison Crowding." *The Annuals*, 478:86–99.

Kandel, D.B. (1980). "Drug and Drinking Behavior Among Youth." *Annual Review of Sociology*. New York: Annual Reviews, Inc.

Kaplan, H.B. (1975). *Self-Attitude and Deviant Behavior*. Pacific Palisade, California: Goodyear Publishing Co.

Kaplan, H.B., S.S. Martin, and C. Robbins (1984). "Pathways to Adolescent Drug Use: Self-Derogation, Peer Influence, Weakening of Social Controls, and Early Substance Abuse." *Journal of Health and Social Behavior* 25(3), 270–289.

Krahn, A.B., Gary Arling and Kenneth Lerner (1988). *SJS: Strategies for Juvenile Supervision*. Unpublished.

Krisberg, Barry (1989). Juvenile Justice: A Critical Examination (draft). San Francisco: NCCD.

Krisberg, Barry (1980). "Utility of Process Evaluation: Crime and Delinquency Programs." In M.W. Klein and K.S. Tielman, *Handbook of Criminal Justice Evaluation*. Beverly Hills, California: Sage Publications.

Krisberg, Barry, et al. (1988). *The Impact of Juvenile Court Sanctions*. San Francisco: NCCD.

Krisberg, Barry, James Austin, and Patricia A. Steele (1989). *Unlocking Juvenile Corrections*. San Francisco: NCCD.

Krisberg, Barry, Orlando Rodriguez, Audrey Bakke, Deborah Neuenfeldt, and Patricia Steele (1989). *Demonstration of Postadjudication Nonresidential Intensive Supervision Programs: Assessment Report*. San Francisco: National Council on Crime and Delinquency.

Lerman, Paul (1975). *Community Treatment and Social Control*. Chicago: University of Chicago Press.

Markley, Greg, and Michael Eisenberg (1986). The Texas Board of Pardons and Paroles Case Management System (draft). Austin: Board of Pardons and Paroles.

Meehl, Paul E. (1954). *Clinical Versus Statistical Prediction*. Minneapolis: University of Minnesota.

Murray, Charles, and Louis Cox (1979). *Beyond Probation*. Beverly Hills, California: Sage Publications.

National Council on Crime and Delinquency (1987). *The Impact of Juvenile Court Intervention*. San Francisco: NCCD.

National Institute of Corrections. "Model Probation/Parole Management System." Washington, D.C.: NIC.

O'Leary, Vincent, and Todd Clear (1984). *Directions for Community Corrections in the 1990's.* Washington, D.C.: U.S. Department of Justice, National Institute of Corrections.

Program sites visited by NCCD

Associated Marine Institutes, Inc.—Tampa, Florida
Contact: Robert Weaver, Executive Vice President, 813–963–3344
The Associated Marine Institutes (AMI) is a network of affiliated residential and nonresidential programs in seven States. The programs focus on remedial education and training in marine activities such as scuba diving, sailing, and boating. The focus is on marine activities demonstrates that youth who are engaged in interesting and challenging tasks can be steered away from delinquent behavior.

Firestone Community Day Center School—Los Angeles, California
Contact: Mary Ann Greene, Probation Director, 213–586–6401
This alternative school is a cooperative effort of the local education and probation departments for youth on probation and aftercare. The focus is on education, but a full-time probation officer with casework responsibility for the students is onsite.

Hennepin County Surveillance Program—Minneapolis, Minnesota
Contact: Jim Seward, Correctional Unit Supervisor, 612–348–3673
The probation department operates this surveillance program, which features frequent contacts and strict adherence to court-ordered conditions of probation. A team makes contact with each juvenile two to six times daily. Staffed with Two shifts, 7 days a week, 365 days a year, the program emphasizes internal consistency and meticulous logging of juvenile activities.

Kentfields Rehabilitation Program—Grand Rapids, Michigan
Contact: Michael Robinson, Director, 616–774–3242
This court-administered program combines classroom education and community service with gradual relaxation of strict probation requirements in an aftercare component. The program operates on a behavioral modification system where positive behavior in the home, community, and school is reinforced through a "token economy" system. Points earned are redeemable for money, and these weekly paychecks are a unique component of the program.

The KEY Program, Inc.—Framingham, Massachusetts
Contact: William Little, Executive Director, 508–877–3690
The KEY Program provides a wide range of residential and nonresidential services. The Outreach and Tracking Program includes daily contacts with youth and family and referrals for services. Tracking Plus has a short residential stay prior to the intensive nonresidential component. At KEY, line workers stay a maximum of 14 months, ensuring that high-energy staff are providing direct services, but extensive training and management and consistency of supervision are required to maintain program integrity.

Lucas County Intensive Supervision Unit—Toledo, Ohio
Contact: Sandy Strong, ISU Supervisor, 419–249–6663

This four-phase program is operated by the juvenile court's probation department. The program begins with house arrest; freedom increases as the youth's behavior warrants. Restitution and community service are required of all participants. The Intensive Supervision Unit has strong judicial and community support. Careful planning and development involving a variety of juvenile justice actors occurred before program implementation, accounting, in part, for this support.

Pennsylvania Intensive Probation Supervision—Harrisburg, Pennsylvania
Contact: Keith Snyder, Juvenile Court Consultant, Juvenile Court Judges Commission, 717–787–6910
Ruth Williams, Juvenile Justice Program Manager, Pennsylvania Commission on Crime and Delinquency, 717–787–8559
The Pennsylvania Intensive Probation Supervision Programs began when two State agencies worked together to provide startup funding and establish basic program standards for county probation departments. Oversight is provided by the two State agencies. State standards require frequent contacts with the youth, the family, and school, while the specific operational design varies by county.

Ramsey County Intensive Supervision Project—St. Paul, Minnesota
Contact: James Hayes, Juvenile Division Director, 612–298–6934
This court-operated program emphasizes strict adherence to court-ordered conditions. The three-phase program lasts 90 to 120 days and includes home detention at the onset followed by a period of restricted activities. Staff assigned to branch probation offices provide for ease of access and better understanding of the neighborhood. The individual flavor of each office is considered a program strength, although program consistency is difficult to maintain.

Specialized Gang Supervision Program—Los Angeles, California
Contact: Ernie Castro, SGSP Director, 818–575–4003
High-profile gang members are supervised in the community by a special unit of Los Angeles County probation officers. The program supervises both juveniles and young adult offenders to provide continuity in fighting the Los Angeles gang problem. The goal is to reduce gang-related violence through close surveillance and swift court action for violations.

Wayne County Intensive Probation Program—Detroit, Michigan
Contact: Kathleen VandenBrulle, IPP Supervisor, 313–577–9426
Screening occurs in this court-administered program after a juvenile has been committed to the State. Upon acceptance, juveniles are referred to one of three programs for supervision and services. One program operated by probation, features small caseloads and frequent contacts. Private providers operate the In-Home program, which has a family treatment focus, and the State Ward Diversion program, a day treatment program with onsite education and counseling. Research suggests all three are as successful as institutionalization in reducing recidivism.

■ Researchers
■ Planners
■ Policymakers

*M*ore detailed information about this study and issues surrounding juvenile intensive supervision is available through the Juvenile Justice Clearinghouse.

The full 89-page report *Juvenile Intensive Supervision: An Assessment* discusses in detail the study's findings and its design and research methodologies. The full report is useful for conducting further research, making planning decisions, or drafting policy.

For further information on this or other juvenile justice topics, call the Juvenile Justice Clearinghouse at
800–638–8736.

Publications From OJJDP

The following lists OJJDP publications available from the Juvenile Justice Clearinghouse. To obtain copies, call or write:

Juvenile Justice Clearinghouse
P.O. Box 6000
Rockville, MD 20850
800–638–8736

Most OJJDP publications are available free of charge from the Clearinghouse; requests for more than 10 documents or those from individuals outside the United States require payment for postage and handling. To obtain information on payment procedures or to speak to a juvenile justice information specialist about additional services offered, contact the Juvenile Justice Clearinghouse Monday through Friday, 8:30 a.m. to 7:00 p.m., e.t.

Delinquency Prevention

Education in the Law: Promoting Citizenship in the Schools. 1990, NCJ 125548.

Family Life, Delinquency, and Crime: A Policymaker's Guide. 1994, NCJ 140517.

Mobilizing Community Support for Law-Related Education. 1989, NCJ 118217, $9.75.

OJJDP and Boys and Girls Clubs of America: Public Housing and High-Risk Youth. 1991, NCJ 128412.

Preserving Families To Prevent Delinquency. 1992, NCJ 136397.

Strengthening America's Families: Promising Parenting Strategies for Delinquency Prevention. 1993, NCJ 140781, $9.15.

Missing and Exploited Children

America's Missing and Exploited Children— Their Safety and Their Future. 1986, NCJ 100581.

Child Abuse: Prelude to Delinquency? 1985, NCJ 104275, $7.10.

The Compendium of the North American Symposium on International Child Abduction: How To Handle International Child Abduction Cases. 1993, NCJ 148137, $17.50.

Investigator's Guide to Missing Child Cases: For Law Enforcement Officers Locating Missing Children. 1987, NCJ 108768.

Missing, Abducted, Runaway, and Thrownaway Children in America, First Report: Numbers and Characteristics, National Incidence Studies (Full Report). 1990, NCJ 123668, $14.40.

Missing Children: Found Facts. 1990, NCJ 130916.

Obstacles to the Recovery and Return of Parentally Abducted Children. 1994, NCJ 143458.

Obstacles to the Recovery and Return of Parentally Abducted Children (Full Report). 1993, NCJ 144535, $22.80.

OJJDP Annual Report on Missing Children. 1990, NCJ 130582.

Parental Abductors: Four Interviews (Video). 1993, NCJ 147866, $12.50.

Sexual Exploitation of Missing Children: A Research Review. 1988, NCJ 114273.

Stranger Abduction Homicides of Children. 1989, NCJ 115213.

Status Offenders

Assessing the Effects of the Deinstitutionalization of Status Offenders. 1989, NCJ 115211.

Runaways in Juvenile Courts. 1990, NCJ 124881.

Law Enforcement

Drug Recognition Techniques: A Training Program for Juvenile Justice Professionals. 1990, NCJ 128795.

Evaluation of the Habitual, Serious, and Violent Juvenile Offender Program, Executive Summary. 1986, NCJ 105230.

Innovative Law Enforcement Training Programs: Meeting State and Local Needs. 1991, NCJ 131735.

Law Enforcement Custody of Juveniles (Video). 1992, NCJ 137387, $13.50.

Law Enforcement Policies and Practices Regarding Missing Children and Homeless Youth. 1993, NCJ 145644.

Law Enforcement Policies and Practices Regarding Missing Children and Homeless Youth (Full Report). 1993, NCJ 143397, $13.00.

Targeting Serious Juvenile Offenders Can Make a Difference. 1988, NCJ 114218.

Courts

The Child Victim as a Witness. 1989, NCJ 118315.

Court Careers of Juvenile Offenders. 1988, NCJ 110854, $8.40.

Helping Victims and Witnesses in the Juvenile Justice System: A Program Handbook. 1991, NCJ 139731, $15.00.

Juvenile Court Property Cases. 1990, NCJ 125625.

Juvenile Court Statistics, 1991. 1994, NCJ 147487.

Offenders in Juvenile Court, 1990. 1993, NCJ 145128.

Restitution

Guide to Juvenile Restitution. 1985, NCJ 098466, $12.50.

Liability and Legal Issues in Juvenile Restitution. 1990, NCJ 115405.

National Trends in Juvenile Restitution Programming. 1989, NCJ 115214.

Restitution Experience in Youth Employment: A Monograph and Training Guide to Jobs Components. 1989, NCJ 115404.

Victim-Offender Mediation in the Juvenile Justice System. 1990, NCJ 120976.

Corrections

American Probation and Parole Association's Drug Testing Guidelines and Practices for Juvenile Probation and Parole Agencies. 1992, NCJ 136450.

Conditions of Confinement: Juvenile Detention and Corrections Facilities, Research Summary. 1994, NCJ 141873.

Desktop Guide to Good Juvenile Probation Practice. 1991, NCJ 128218.

Juveniles Taken Into Custody: Fiscal Year 1991 Report. 1993, NCJ 145746.

National Juvenile Custody Trends: 1978– 1989. 1992, NCJ 131649.

National Survey of Reading Programs for Incarcerated Juvenile Offenders. 1993, NCJ 144017, $6.75.

OJJDP: Conditions of Confinement Teleconference (Video). 1993, NCJ 147531, $14.00.

OJJDP Helps States Remove Juveniles From Adult Jails and Lockups. 1990, NCJ 126869.

Private-Sector Corrections Program for Juveniles: Paint Creek Youth Center. 1988, NCJ 113214.

Privatizing Juvenile Probation Services: Five Local Experiences. 1989, NCJ 121507.

Public Juvenile Facilities: Children in Custody 1989. 1991, NCJ 127189.

Reduced Recidivism and Increased Employment Opportunity Through Research-Based Reading Instruction. 1993, NCJ 141324, $7.70.

General Juvenile Justice

Breaking the Code (Video). 1993, NCJ 146604, $20.65.

Comprehensive Strategy for Serious, Violent, and Chronic Juvenile Offenders. 1993, NCJ 143453.

Gang Suppression and Intervention: An Assessment. 1994, NCJ 146494, $20.20.

Gould-Wysinger Awards (1992): Mark of Achievement. 1993, NCJ 142730.

Gould-Wysinger Awards (1993): A Tradition of Excellence. 1994, NCJ 146840.

Guide to the Data Sets in the National Juvenile Court Data Archive. 1991, NCJ 132073.

Gun Acquisition and Possession in Selected Juvenile Samples. 1993, NCJ 145326.

Habitual Juvenile Offenders: Guidelines for Citizen Action and Public Responses. 1991, NCJ 141235.

Innovative Community Partnerships: Working Together for Change. 1994, NCJ 147483.

Juvenile Justice. Volume 1, Number 1, Spring/Summer 1993, NCJ 141870.

Law-Related Education For Juvenile Justice Settings. 1993, NCJ 147063, $13.20.

Minorities and the Juvenile Justice System. 1993, NCJ 145849.

Minorities and the Juvenile Justice System (Full Report). 1993, NCJ 139556, $11.50.

National Juvenile Justice Statistics Assessment: An Agenda for Action. 1989, NCJ 119764.

Office of Juvenile Justice and Delinquency Prevention Brochure. 1993, NCJ 144527.

Retarding America—The Imprisonment of Potential (Video). 1993, NCJ 146605, $12.95.

Study of Tribal and Alaska Native Juvenile Justice Systems. 1992, NCJ 148217, $17.20.

Urban Delinquency and Substance Abuse: Initial Findings. 1994, NCJ 143454.

Urban Delinquency and Substance Abuse: Technical Report and Appendices. 1993, NCJ 146416, $25.60.

Violent Juvenile Offenders: An Anthology. 1984, NCJ 095108, $28.00.